C0-AWT-237

THE
UNIVERSITY OF WINNIPEG
PORTAGE & BALMORAL
WINNIPEG 2, MAN.   CANADA

DISCARDED

TENNYSON'S USE OF THE BIBLE

PR
5592
.P5 R6
1968

TENNYSON'S USE OF THE BIBLE

by

Edna Moore Robinson

GORDIAN PRESS,
NEW YORK
1968

Originally Published 1917

Reprinted 1968

Library of Congress Catalogue Card Number 68-57381

Published by GORDIAN PRESS

THIS STUDY IS DEDICATED

TO

JAMES WILSON BRIGHT

TABLE OF CONTENTS

PREFACE

In his essay on Dryden, Macaulay incidentally characterizes the English Bible as " a book which, if everything else in our language should perish would alone suffice to show the whole extent of its beauty and power." The statement carries more of accuracy than of hyperbole. For the English Bible contains almost every species of literature and contains each species in varied forms. The historic books are fine examples of simple narration. They are impartial and objective in quality and often dramatic, vivid, and picturesque. They run the whole scale from the naïve biographies of the patriarchs to the dignified annals of the Kings. The prophets afford examples of eloquence which in richness of diction, in pathos, and in austere rebuke have never been surpassed. The lyric outbursts of the *Psalms* compare favorably with any other similar utterance of the troubled or gladdened heart. The idyl of *Ruth* was included in one of the volumes of " Little Classics " by a critical editor whose selections were much commended. Among elegies the *Lamentations of Jeremiah* have a secure position. Popular and laconic wisdom is constantly quoted from the book of *Proverbs*. *Ecclesiastes* is a philosophic meditation. *Job* is an Epic,—" The Epic of the Inner Life " as Prof. Genung styles it. And finally, the *Song of Songs* reveals something very much like the shifting scenes and dialogues of the drama. Many biblical critics place it in that class.

If we take into consideration the various general qualities of literature, the Bible still affords a broad vision. W. Trail, in his *Literary Characteristics and Achievements of the Bible*,[1] devotes instructive chapters, each with numerous sub-headings, to The Figurative, The Sublime, The Pathetic, The Picturesque, and The Poetic in the Scriptures. A still further com-

[1] Cincinnati, 1864.

v

prehensiveness is to be observed in the relative maturity of expression. The style of the biblical writers varies from the simplicity of childhood to the elaborateness of the man who knows rhetoric and the value of stylistic expressions. Professor J. H. Gardiner [2] effectively contrasts the story, in *First Samuel,* of David killing Goliath with the story, in the *Acts,* of the viper which fastened on Paul's hand at Malta. It is a far cry from the short clauses, the simple connectives, and the unpremeditated simplicity of the former to the finish and grace of the latter. It is still farther to the involved sentences and the sidetracking clauses of the speeches and epistles of Paul. No one can rise from the reading of this admirable study without feeling a new and stronger sense of the innumerable kinds and grades of literary expression contained in the Bible.

But tho the English Bible is a library of writing containing literature of every species and in every stage of development it is, nevertheless, a single volume. It is a translation. The translation is so faithful to the original tongues and writings that in the main it preserves their variety. But it is, after all, a translation into one language and a translation into that language when it was highly developed. When the English Bible was made, good English, as Matthew Arnold says in the introduction to his *Great Prophecy of Israel's Restoration,* " was in the air." " Get a body of learned divines,"—so he goes on,—" and set them down to translate, the right meaning they might often have difficulty with, but the right style was pretty well sure to come of itself." The sixteenth century which developed the wonderful English of Shakespeare was the century during which the English Bible gradually acquired its greatest idiomatic beauty, grace, and power of style and expression. Tyndale's version of the New Testament was published in 1525. The people were eager for the Bible-truth, and the phrases and idioms of Tyndale passed into the common stock of the speech of the people. Good writers took them, as if by

[2] J. H. Gardiner, *The Bible as English Literature.* New York, Charles Scribner's Sons, 1906.

instinct, from the speech of the people and wove them into their productions. It is doubtless difficult in many cases to say whether a given phrase comes from the colloquial speech or from the English Bible. It may in reality come from both. But oftener than is always realized it originally came from Tyndale or Coverdale. Thus the English Bible was, in all the circumstances, sure to be good English as well as magnificently diversified English. It was sure to be largely Saxon, for the speech of the people and the century was, in the main, guiltless of foreign derivatives, at least of those with the later and artificial colorings. It was sure to be concrete, because of the characteristic concreteness of the original. It was sure to be metaphorical for all Hebrew words even those for spiritual ideas have an evident·physical meaning or connection. It was sure to be forcible, for the lash of an active conscience drove it on. It was even sure to be rhythmical, for altho it lacked rime and meter, it had parallelism which was the rhythmic "heaving and sinking of the heart" reproduced in balanced clauses, and it had, moreover, a fine onomatapoetic quality.

It is not surprising, therefore, to find that the Bible has had a great influence upon English writers. John Ruskin acknowledged his indebtedness: "To that discipline [of reading the English Bible and memorizing extended portions of it] I owe . . . the best part of my taste in literature . . . ; once knowing the 32nd of Deuteronomy, the 119th Psalm, the 15th of 1 Corinthians, the Sermon on the Mount, and most of the Apocalyse, every syllable by heart, . . . it was not possible for me, even in the foolishest times of youth, to write entirely superficial or formal English."[3] Tennyson declared that "the Bible ought to be read, were it only for the sake of the grand English in which it is written, an education in itself."[4] Coleridge (*Table-Talk,* June 14, 1830) believed that "Intense study of the Bible will keep any writer from being vulgar in point of style." A number of similar testimonials have been collected

---

[3] *Fors Clavigera,* I, x, 5.   [4] *Memoir,* I, 308, note 1.

by Professor Cook [5] from many different writers. But perhaps
the most striking example he cites of the power of the Bible to
influence an author's style is that of John Bunyan: "When a
writer, with a native vigor, lightness, and rapidity of his own,
has become wholly permeated, as it were, with the thought and
diction of the Bible, . . . we have from him such a clear, simple, and picturesque style as that of Bunyan." [6]

No author's use of the English Bible is more instructive than
that of Tennyson. The reason for this lies both in the completeness and in the limitation of it. Tennyson knows his Bible
as completely as Bunyan, but unlike Milton, Browning, and
others, he has no poem on a biblical subject. He makes no use
of poetical figures derived from the original Greek or Hebrew
as Milton was constantly doing.[7] He uses the English Bible
only. It furnished him with material for artistic portrayal
thruout his whole career. The various rhetorical devices by
which he made his use of Scripture effective have been briefly
indicated in the Introduction. It is not the purpose of this
paper to give them in full at this time. Nor am I attempting
to do the same thing for Tennyson that Bishop Wordsworth has
done for Shakespeare or Mrs. Machen for Browning.[8] There
is no question here as to the indebtedness of Tennyson to the

---

[5] Albert S. Cook, *The Bible and English Prose Style*. Boston, D. C.
Heath & Co., 1892.

[6] *Op. cit.*, Intro. xiv.

[7] For example, Milton (*P. L.*, I, 21) selects his word "brooding" with
conscious conformity to the Hebrew מְרַחֶפֶת (cf. John P. Peters, *Journal
of Bibl. Literature*, xxx and xxxiii). Satan is in Hebrew 'enemy' (*P. L.*,
I, 81 f.). Birds and animals (*P. L.*, v, 197, cf. vii, 451), are called "living
souls," which is warranted by the use of נֶפֶשׁ חַיָּה at both *Gen.* II, 7 and I, 20.
Angels are called "ardours" (*P. L.*, v, 249, cf. 277 and *Isa.* vi) because
Seraphim in Hebrew are "burning ones." Urania (*P. L.*, vii, 5 f.) is
'Heavenly One' (Greek Οὐρανία). The corrupt clergy (*Lycidas*, 119)
are "blind mouths" (see Ruskin, *Sesame and Lilies*, I, 22). David Masson
has additional observations of this character in the notes of his edition
of *The Poetical Works of Milton* (1890).

[8] Charles Wordsworth, *Shakespeare's Knowledge and Use of the Bible*,
London, Smith, Elder & Co., 1880; Mrs. Minnie Gresham Machen, *The Bible
in Browning*, New York, Macmillian Co., 1903.

thought and sentiments of Scripture. The single attempt is to discover from Tennyson's use of Scripture the successive and orderly stages of his artistic and poetic development. Here is a poet who used biblical phrases and images in one way in his earliest lines, who used them in another way in subsequent poems, and in still other ways in productions that were later and later yet. If the following pages have any new value it lies in exhibiting the orderly development and progress of a great poet's genius by showing that progress and development as seen in the successive stages of his artistic use of the English Bible. The Bible is familiar to all. Tennyson's other material is less familiar. The way of using the familiar, once clearly seen, is a key to the use of the unfamiliar. It is an outline of it. It is a clear path thru the beautiful forest. Seen as a whole it is a bird's-eye view of the total landscape of a great artist's far-stretching career.

INTRODUCTION

Some years ago Tennyson's frequent and effective use of the English Bible began to attract my attention. Out of this interest grew the idea of making a complete list of the late Laureate's references to Scripture. The practical result took the form of two tables. One of these follows the order of biblical book, chapter, and verse. The other follows the final published order of Tennyson's poems. The total number of citations in these tables is about two thousand. To print them with even a slight indication of their verbal connections would require many pages. The limitations of this study evidently forbid such an attempt at this time. Specimens will, however, be given at the close of this introduction.

After a while the idea occurred to me of arranging the more important references into a chain running thru the entire Bible; each link would thus represent a single citation by the poet of some scriptural passage. The fact that the citations fall so close together as to recall or at least suggest almost the entire contents of the Bible is a striking testimony to the prevalence of Scripture in the poet's pages. This scriptural chain proved very lengthy. Two brief sections of it, however, one from *Genesis* and the other from *Matthew,* may be given here by way of illustration. These, taken together with the specimens from the reference tables, will suffice to show how thickly set the pages of Tennyson are with occurrences of biblical import.

Beginning then with the very first chapter of *Genesis* we see the spirit of God move over the primeval deep.[1] Light follows the creative fiat.[2] In the sixth cycle nature moulds man [3] in the divine likeness [4] and assigns him dominion over creation.[5]

[1] *De Profundis*, II, i.
[2] *Princess*, III, 306.
[3] *Two Voices*, 16-18.

[4] *De Profundis*, II, ii.
[5] *Two Voices*, 20 f.

1

The four rivers [6] flow through the garden [7] of Eden.[8] The mist keeps it green [9] even without any rain.[10] There are no thorns under the grateful shadows of the huge trees.[11] Mazily the brooks murmur.[12] Everything is plentiful and good.[13] Adam divinely moulded out of dust [14] keeps the garden [15] and Eve is there in her snowy beauty,[16] both of them unfallen and divine.[17] Happy is Adam's embrace of Eve,[18] for she was made for him,[19] bone of his bone and flesh of his flesh.[20] There is no shame of nakedness [21] and the bright moon glows upon their bridal bower.[22]

Then comes the fall.[23] The serpent creeps in [24] and stirs the vice that ruins.[25] The " apple " is plucked [26] and the expulsion from Paradise follows.[27] The days of the curse come with their toil [28] and their sweat,[29] the days of the trampled serpent and the wounded heel,[30] and the return of man's dust to that of earth.[31] The cry of Abel's blood is heard,[32] and though Cain declares he is not his brother's keeper,[33] he feels his punishment beyond bearing,[34] and with the preserving mark upon his forehead [35] wanders off to the land of Nod.[36] The echo of his crime is still heard in the song of Lamech.[37]

The dim line of patriarchs appears in Methusaleh,[38] and Noah with his ark.[39] The penalty of the corruption of the

[6] *Geraint and Enid*, 763 f.
[7] *Gardener's Daughter*, 187.
[8] *Happy*, 33.
[9] *Geraint and Enid*, 768 f.
[10] *Geraint and Enid*, 770.
[11] *Maud*, I, xviii, 625.
[12] *Milton*.
[13] *Enoch Arden*, 557.
[14] *Introduction to Palace of Art*, 17 ff.
[15] *Lady Clara Vere de Vere*.
[16] *Maud*, I, xviii, 625.
[17] *Happy*, 33.
[18] *Day Dream, L'Envoi*, 253-7.
[19] *Edwin Morris*.
[20] *Rizpah*.
[21] *Vision of Sin*, 190.
[22] *In Memoriam*, CXXXI.
[23] *Two Voices*, 358-360.

[24] *Foresters*, II, i, 93.
[25] *Merlin and Vivien*, 359.
[26] *Becket*, III, i, 91.
[27] *Becket, Prolog*, 368.
[28] *Two Voices*, 229.
[29] *Foresters*, IV, i, 139-142.
[30] *Locksley Hall*, 60 yr., 242.
[31] *Queen Mary*, III, v, 35.

[32] *Maud*, II, i, 34.
[33] *Becket*, I, iv, 175.
[34] *Harold*, v, ii, 111.
[35] *Queen Mary*, III, ii, 34.
[36] *Becket*, I, iv, 185.
[37] *Maud*, II, iv, 185.
[38] *Promise of May*, I, 344.
[39] *In Memoriam*, XII.

sons of God and daughters of men [40] is the breaking up of the
great deeps [41] in the deluge.[42] Babel is builded and its tongues
are confounded.[43] Lot's wife is stiff with encrusted salt.[44]
Esau's rough hand [45] is no match for the finer one of Jacob who
sees his ladder-of-heaven [46] with its ascending and descending
angels,[47] meets Rachel by the palmy well,[48] serves seven years
for her,[49] and returning with wealth has his night struggle [50]
with the unknown power [51] which blesses him.[52] His fear that
his gray hairs will be brought in sorrow to the grave [53] is done
away and his dying blessing upon Joseph is bounded by the
everlasting hills alone.[54]

In *Matthew* we find the wise men with their gifts [55] following the flying star to Bethlehem.[56] Joseph is warned in his
dream.[57] John the Baptist announces the kingdom of heaven [58]
and Him whose fan will purge His floor,[59] and who will garner
the wheat, and burn the tares with unquenchable fire.[60] After
his fast of forty days [61] Jesus is tempted by Satan to fall down
and worship him.[62] He calls Peter and Andrew to be fishers
of men.[63] He begins the Sermon on the Mount with its beati-
tudes: Blessed are the poor in spirit.[64] The meek shall inherit
the earth.[65] The persecuted have their reward in heaven.[66]
The salt must not lose its savor.[67] He comes not to destroy but
to fulfill.[68] His word will endure when heaven and earth
pass,[69] and the fires of hell [70] await him who says to his brother

[40] *Aylmer's Field*, 44.
[41] *Becket*, v, iii, 24.
[42] *Sonnet*, x.
[43] *Princess*, iv, 59, 466-7.
[44] *Princess*, vi, 224.
[45] *Godiva*.
[46] *By an Evolutionist, Old Age*, 2.
[47] *Palace of Art*, 143.
[48] *Aylmer's Field*, 679.
[49] *Promise of May*, ii, 59-60.
[50] *To*—('*Clear-headed friend*').
[51] *In Memoriam*, xcvi.
[52] *In Memoriam*, cxxiv.
[53] *Aylmer's Field*, 777.
[54] *Dream of Fair Women*, 226.
[55] *Morte d'Arthur*, 283 f.

[56] *Holy Grail*, 452.
[57] *Harold*, i, ii, 55.
[58] *Church Warden*, x.
[59] *Queen Mary*, iii, iv, 227.
[60] *Queen Mary*, v, v, 69.
[61] *Harold*, iv, iii, 101.
[62] *Becket*, iii, iii, 213.
[63] *Harold*, ii, i, 21.
[64] *Aylmer's Field*, 754.
[65] *The Dreamer*.
[66] *Queen Mary*, v, ii, 66.
[67] *Maud*, i, ii, 78.
[68] *Queen Mary*, iii, iii, 121.
[69] *Lover's Tale*, i, 68.
[70] *Princess*, v, 444.

" Thou fool." Injunctions follow: Agree with thine adversary quickly.[71] Look not on a woman.[72] Cut off the offending hand.[73] To him that smites on one cheek turn the other.[74] Hate not your enemy,[75] but love and bless him.[76] Pray that the Father's name be hallowed [77] and His will be done.[78] Serve not Mammon.[79] The lilies toil not [80] but God clothes them with better apparel than Solomon's.[81] Let each day's evil suffice without foreboding for the next.[82] As ye measure it shall be meted to you.[83] Cast no pearls to swine [84] lest they turn and rend you.[85] Knock and it shall be opened.[86] Narrow is the way to life.[87] There are no figs from thistles or grapes from thorns.[88] He that hears and does, builds on the rock; [89] he that hears and does not, builds on sand; [90] and all these sayings are spoken with authority.[91]

In converse fashion a running paraphrase of each poem might be given which would show the exact nature and extent of the Scripture it contained. This would also enable the reader to compare the usage of Scripture in any one poem with that in any other. As an example of how this might be done the following synopsis of the biblical element in *Merlin and Vivien* is here given. To follow this method with all the poems would also require many more pages than are available at this time.

Vivien scornfully likens the vows of Arthur's Knights to those of the angels who neither marry nor are given in marriage.[92] She feels the perfect hate for them which, like perfect love, casts out fear.[93] Arthur himself is not pure, for there

---

[71] *Becket*, II, ii, 234.
[72] *Queen Mary*, I, v, 253.
[73] *Queen Mary*, IV, iii, 413.
[74] *Queen Mary*, I, i, 82.
[75] *Locksley Hall*, 60 yr., 94.
[76] *Akbar's Dream*, 74.
[77] *De Profundis, Human Cry*.
[78] *May Queen, Conclusion*, 10.
[79] *Maud*, I, i, 46.
[80] *Lotos Eaters*, 36, 37.
[81] *Becket*, III, i, 27.
[82] *Foresters*, I, i, 239.

[83] *Aylmer's Field*, 316.
[84] *Sir John Oldcastle*, 110.
[85] *Becket*, II, ii, 89.
[86] *Becket*, v, iii, 34.
[87] *Church Warden*, IV.
[88] *Riflemen Form*.
[89] *Edwin Morris*, 6.
[90] *Becket*, III, iii, 39.
[91] *Coming of Arthur*, 260.
[92] *Matthew*, XXII, 30.
[93] *1 John*, IV, 18.

is no being pure, as Holy Writ declares.[94]   Both Arthur
and Vivien, tho in different ways, leavened their associ-
ates.[95]   When she went from the Court she left death behind
her.[96]   Merlin likened her curiosity to that of Eve by which
mankind was originally ruined.[97]   She herself regarded Percivale not as a spotless lamb of Christ [98] but rather as some black
wether of Saint Satan's fold.[99]   Merlin mitigated her censure by
referring to the case of the Psalmist.[100]   But when she persisted
in letting her tongue rage like a fire among the noblest names [101]
Merlin rebuked her for judging all nature from her feet of
clay.[102]   Soon, however, she fell to wailing that her own affec-
tions were being used to stab her to the heart, seethed like the
kid in its mother's milk.[103]

The passages of Scripture used by Tennyson are distinctly
and individually recognizable.   Yet his art never leaves them
as he finds them.   After long study and several attempts at
classification I found certain rhetorical devices or practices
of treatment by which he used Scripture so as to make it speci-
ally effective for his poetical purposes.   These devices show the
student of English composition how ordinary images and
phrases may be given an enhanced effectiveness.   An added
value is also given to this study by the fact that Tennyson employed similar rhetorical devices and practices with reference
to his art in general.   This detailed study of his rhetorical
usage of biblical material thus serves as a kind of index or illustration of his minor artistic methods in general.   This may be
a sufficient justification for presenting at this point a skeleton
outline, with a few brief examples under each division, of the
various artistic methods referred to above.   A sharp distinction, however, must be made between this skeleton or outline
of rhetorical methods and the larger features or stages of the

[94] *Romans*, III, 10; *Proverbs*, XX, 9; *Job*, XXV, 5 f.
[95] *Matthew*, XIII, 33; *Galatians*, V, 9.
[96] *2 Kings*, IV, 39 f.   [100] *2 Samuel*, XI.
[97] *Genesis*, III, 1-6.   [101] *James*, III, 6.
[98] *John*, XXI, 15; *1 Peter*, I, 19.   [102] *Daniel*, II, 33.
[99] *Revelation*, II, 9.   [103] *Exodus*, XXIII, 19.

poet's use of biblical material which will be treated in the main
body of this study.   These features or stages are chronological
and represent successive periods of artistic development.   The
outline of rhetorical uses, on the contrary, represents, in the
main, methods in use thruout the entire range of the poet's
published works.   The principle of division here is not chronological and progressive, but rhetorical and artistic merely.

1.   As may be noticed first, Tennyson intensified scriptural
expressions, by making them more concrete or by giving
them a livelier action or more vivid coloring.   Jacob's ladder
reached to heaven, but Tennyson hangs it upon a single star.[104]
The fountains of the great deep are not only broken up as in
the Bible but they also hiss against the sun.[105]   Michael fight-
ing against Satan becomes Michael trampling Satan.[106]   The
worm that never dies becomes the scorpion worm that twists in
hell and stings itself to everlasting death.[107]

2.   A second method which Tennyson employed very effectively was that of reversal.   He frequently reversed the order
or meaning of a scriptural expression or gave it an unexpected
change of application.   It is to Death, not Christ, that the
senses say, as they crown him, " Omega, thou art Lord." [108]
In the days of bloody Mary it is ignorance, not wisdom, that was
seen crying in the streets.[109]   Solomon may come to Sheba
yet [110] and man be the one to ask hard questions and woman
the one able to answer them.[111]   The monks instead of selling
all they have and giving to the poor, take all the poor have and
give it to themselves.[112]   Mary's new commandment is " Thou
shalt do murder." [113]   The beautiful cross presented to Rosa-

---

[104] *By an Evolutionist, Old Age,* 2; *Genesis,* xxviii, 12.
[105] *Becket,* v, iii, 24; *Genesis,* vii, 11.
[106] *Last Tournament,* 668; *Revelation,* xii, 7-9.
[107] *Last Tournament,* 450 f; *Isaiah,* lxvi, 24.
[108] *Two Voices,* 278; *Revelation,* i, 8.
[109] *Queen Mary,* iv, iii, 242; *Proverbs,* i, 20 f.
[110] *Princess,* ii, 328; *1 Kings,* x, 1.
[111] *Princess* ii, 324-334; *1 Kings,* iv, 31; *1 Kings,* x, 1.
[112] *Foresters,* iii, i, 103; *Matthew,* xix, 21.
[113] *Queen Mary,* iii, i, 242; *Matthew,* xix, 18.

mond is to remind her not only of Him who died for her but also of Henry who lives for her.[114]

3. In addition to intensifying and reversing scriptural words and conceptions, Tennyson is found comparing non-scriptural things with scriptural in such a way as to give the outside thing greater clearness or greater beauty. Edith was fairer than Rachel by the palmy well, or Ruth among the fields of corn, and the equal of the angel that said " Hail." [115] The Lord in afflicting Ulrich with leprosy has set upon him a crueller mark than Cain's.[116] Cyril tells his protectors at the institute that they will receive no less royal a welcome when they come to visit him and his friends than the Queen of Sheba did when she went to visit Solomon.[117] Lutterworth where Wiclif was rector is no less important a town than Bethlehem, for in it the word was born again.[118] Not to desire or admire, if one could but learn it, were better than to walk in a garden of spice.[119]

4. The Bible furnishes Tennyson with much material for similes. The leper is at last to stand transfigured like Christ on Hermon hill.[120] To worn-out Harold a snatch of sleep were like the peace of God.[121] The blazing tower of the Red Knight's Castle, like the pulsations of the northern lights, made mountain and lake for half the night glow like the sunrise-redness upon the water which Moab thought was the redness of blood.[122] Lancelot's outraged conscience drove him into wastes and solitudes as the demon did the Gadarene.[123] At young Henry's crowning, John of Salisbury glanced furtively about as " a thief at night who hears a door open and thinks ' The Master.' " [124]

---

[114] *Becket*, II, i, 167; *2 Corinthians*, v, 15.
[115] *Aylmer's Field*, 679 f.; *Genesis*, XXIX, 10; *Ruth*, II; *Luke*, I, 28.
[116] *Happy*, 18; *Genesis*, IV, 15.
[117] *Princess*, II, 330 f.; *1 Kings*, X, 4 f.
[118] *Sir John Oldcastle*, 24 f.; *Micah*, v, 2.
[119] *Maud*, I, iv, 142 f.; *Song of Solomon*, IV, 16.
[120] *Happy*, 38; *Matthew*, XVII, 1 f.
[121] *Harold*, v, i, 104; *Philippians*, IV, 7.
[122] *Last Tournament*, 481 f.; *2 Kings*, III, 20-23.
[123] *Lancelot and Elaine*, 250 f.; *Luke*, VIII, 29.
[124] *Becket*, III, iii, 77-80; *Matthew*, XXIV, 43.

As Jesus reserved the best wine at Cana till the last, so Arthur reserved Lancelot's story of his search for the Holy Grail.[125]

5. After comparisons and similes come metaphors. Here the material is very rich and varied. Childhood is a porch of which the two pillars are parents. If one pillar falls, the burden of care trembles upon the other.[126] To the " new woman " of the intensest type men are an Egypt plague,[127] whose very presence reminds her of her days of bondage and toil in the Egypt of subjection to man.[128] Maud's lover says she has neither savor nor salt,[129] but afterwards declares that the whole inherited sin of the family belongs to her scapegoat brother.[130] If Harold should break his oath the hosts of heaven would send their celestial troops to dash the torch of war among the standing corn of England.[131] Averill's audience should shroud the great sin of separating Edith and Leolin in Pharaoh's darkness.[132] Sir Edward Head, the sour, self-centered conservative, is vexed with a morbid devil in his blood,[133] and any bill that would work changes would be the last drop in his cup of gall.[134] Man superstitiously worships the Baäl of his own worst self [135] and women Molochise their own babes.[136] Becket insists that the customs of the church are Peter's rock,[137] and with grateful assumption accepts the applause of the crowd as praise from the mouths of religious and mental babes and sucklings.[138]

6. In all the foregoing biblical descriptions, comparisons, metaphors, and other rhetorical methods Tennyson writes with

---

[125] *Holy Grail*, 759 f.; *John*, II, 1-10.
[126] *Lover's Tale*, I, 214; *1 Kings*, VII, 21.
[127] *Princess*, v, 417; *Exodus*, VII-XII.
[128] *Princess*, IV, 109 f.; *Exodus*, I, 14.
[129] *Maud*, I, ii, 78; *Song of Solomon*, IV, 16.
[130] *Maud*, I, xiii, 485; *Leviticus*, XVI, 21.
[131] *Harold*, II, ii, 406 f.; *Judges*, XV, 4, 5.
[132] *Aylmer's Field*, 771; *Exodus*, X, 21.
[133] *Walking to the Mail*, 13; *Matthew*, XV, 22.
[134] *Walking to the Mail*, 61; *Matthew*, XXVII, 34.
[135] *Aylmer's Field*, 644; *1 Kings*, XVIII, 28.
[136] *Harold*, I, i, 18; *Leviticus*, XVIII, 21.
[137] *Becket*, I, iii, 13; *Matthew*, XVI, 18.
[138] *Becket*, II, ii, 158; *Psalms*, VIII, 2.

a vivid sense of the details implicitly contained in the scripture images used, tho not directly mentioned in the biblical language itself. This leads to so many effective extensions of scriptural expressions that the practice is worthy of separate mention. It does not connote, of course, a separate rhetorical device coördinate or homogeneous with the preceding ones of simile, metaphor, etc., but refers to a habit or characteristic which pervades all of them alike. The " valley of weeping " has a lower end where there is a grave.[139] The " water wears away the stones " by falling drop by drop [140] upon them and hollowing them out.[141] The " grievous wolves " drag the scattered limbs of the church into their dens.[142] The five belated Virgins find the wedding night to be dark and chill. They have heard of the bridegroom's sweetness and long to kiss his feet and find the light.[143] Our " earthly house of this tabernacle " has Life and Thought as its careless tenants who have gone away leaving the doors and windows open. The shutters should be closed, for the tenants have bought another house in a distant city.[144] Tho the work of purging out the old leaven may in a general way be complete, some of it may still stick to a man's tongue.[145] It is not only in the sweat of his brow but also of his breast, arms, legs, heart, and liver that a man eats the king's venison.[146] When Lazarus in his grave heard Mary weeping outside, was he affected by her tears? Where was he, in fact, during those four days? [147] God moulded man from common clay, but he tempered the mixture with the tears of angels.[148]

Still other categories might be mentioned but what have been

[139] *Promise of May,* III, 186; *Psalms,* LXXXIV, 6.
[140] *Charge of Heavy Brigade, Epilogue,* 59-61; *Job,* XIV, 19.
[141] *Becket,* III, iii, 237 f.; *Job,* XIV, 19.
[142] *Queen Mary,* I, v, 226 f.; *Acts,* XX, 29.
[143] *Guinevere,* 166-177; *Matthew,* XXV, 1 ff.
[144] *The Deserted House; 2 Corinthians,* V, 1.
[145] *Queen Mary,* I, iii, 39; *1 Corinthians,* V, 7.
[146] *Foresters,* IV, i, 139-142; *Genesis,* III, 19.
[147] *In Memoriam,* XXXI; *John,* XI.
[148] *Intro. to Palace of Art,* 17 ff.; *Genesis,* II, 7.

given are sufficient to show the nature of this rhetorical study. It is altogether too extended and detailed to admit of more than a brief indication of it here. In my complete manuscript the number and variety of instances is many times greater. A sentence in the outline given above often corresponds to a whole page in the full treatment. Each category is, moreover, subdivided into several minor categories and numerous and complete examples are cited under each. This rhetorical study is thus, also, a book in itself and cannot of course be included here. These various studies outlined in the preceding pages of this introduction, and here omitted for lack of space, the writer hopes to publish at some future date.

Tenyson made artistic use of Scripture thruout his entire poetical career. He used it in the various rhetorical ways just outlined. But while studying these in detail I became more and more aware of certain larger tones, features, or stages in the poet's methods of dealing with the Bible. It finally occurred to me that these larger modes and attitudes had a definite chronological succession. They evidently coincided with the main divisions or periods of the poet's artistic life and work. This discovery, however simple, has considerable value. Its value would be smaller if Tennyson had used Scripture fitfully or only at certain periods of his career. If he had given himself vigorously at times to biblical subjects the same would be true. But in the case of Tennyson, as contrasted, for example, with Browning, it is the artistic temper and method alone that are in evidence. He has no poems whatever on biblical subjects. Not even *Rizpah* is an exception to this statement. In the Bible, then, we have a single definite variety of material, the artistic use of which Tennyson never abandoned. When a great artist changes his material or his theme, his new subject or new matter may, at least in part, be the cause of his new attitude and method. But where the same material is continuous, the change must be in the artist himself. By following Tennyson's changing uses of the Bible we see more clearly than in any other one way the changes in the man himself and his essential methods.

In the case of Tennyson the need of establishing some such single clue or guide is unusually evident. For Tennyson was constantly going back to poems written years before and revising them by adding, by erasing, by altering, and even by rearranging. The effect is exceedingly confusing to the student of chronological development. To find satire and allegory in a single early and simple idyll seems to indicate that the poet had no specific allegorical period as distinguished from a satirical one or from the period of simplicity. But with the successive periods of artistic uses of Scripture once clearly established, the investigator knows where to suspect the revising hand. The study of the early and successive editions always verifies his suspicions and at the same time makes the stages and periods stand out with greater clearness than ever.

In roughest outline, then, Tennyson's use of the Bible for the purposes of his art may be divided into six successive stages or periods: The Period of Simplicity; the Period of Combination; the Allegorical Period; the Satirical Period; the Dramatic Period; and the Period of Disuse. There are some overlappings, recrudescences, and anticipations; but, on the whole, the divisions are remarkably distinct. They are not distinct like the air-tight chambers of the nautilus which our newer science describes, but resemble, rather, the old-time nautilus of which the divisions were separate enough but had a membraneous tube admitting of subtle transfusions back and forth. Notwithstanding these subtler connections the divisions are sufficiently clear, so long as attention is directed to the main outstanding features. It is hoped that the nature of the six great periods mentioned above and the evidence establishing them are indicated with reasonable plainness in the following pages.

The scope of the present study is limited to artistic stages and methods. But the English Bible is the English nation's religious book. Poetry and religion are closely akin. James Martineau anticipated their ultimate identity. The national religious book has therefore a somewhat intrinsic relation to an English poet. Tennyson's own personal experiences, moreover, vibrated in sensitive sympathy with all the great scientific and theological evolutions and revolutions of the sixty years thru which his poetical work extended. They inevitably affected not only his general relation but also his artistic relation to his religious book. It is also well known that it was along the paths of his religious and biblical faith that his personal sorrows wrought so deeply upon his poetic life. *In Memoriam* is generally considered his greatest work. In that poem he comes to very close quarters not only with the science and philosophy of his day but also with the objective statements and the inward spirit of his Bible. An intense personal relation to the Scriptures comes in to mould and influence his poetic use of the biblical material. Fully to trace the interwoven workings of personal poetic development, of contemporary thought and history, and of individual experiences upon Tennyson's use of the Bible in making his poetry would, of course, be an impossible task. But a mere reference to the complete problem may serve to quicken an interest in the partial study that is offered here.

SPECIMENS OF TABLES

TABLE I

(Following Biblical Order of Book, Chapter, and Verse)

OLD TESTAMENT

Exodus

1:14	The Princess, iv, 109 f.
3:5	The Poet's Mind, ii.
3:8	The Lover's Tale, i, 326.
7-12	The Princess, v, 417.
7:19 (12:22)	Becket, i, iii, 201-4.
9:23	The Promise of May, i, 558.
10:21	Aylmer's Field, 771.
12:22 (7:19)	Becket, i, iii, 201-204.
13:21	Despair, 29.
14:20	The Lover's Tale, i, 290 f.

Leviticus

Numbers

Job

NEW TESTAMENT

John

2 : 1-10 .... The Holy Grail, 759 f.

3 : 16 .... Queen Mary, IV, iii, 95 f.

3 : 17 .... Queen Mary, III, iii, 119.

3 : 29 .... Becket, I, iii, 390.

3 : 30 .... Boädicea.

3 : 35 .... Becket, III, iii, 202.

4 : 10 .... Queen Mary, I, v, 58.

4 : 10 .... Sir John Oldcastle, 124.

4 : 48 .... Guinevere, 272.

6 : 37 .... Queen Mary, IV, iii, 88 f.

6 : 51 .... Becket, I, iv, 257 f.

8 : 1-11 .... Queen Mary, II, ii, 5 f.

8 : 56 .... The Lover's Tale, I, 185 f.

9 : 6 .... The Princess, VII, 312.

10 : 11 .... Harold, III, ii, 99.

10 : 12 .... Becket, I, iii, 302.

10 : 12 f. .... Harold, v, i, 294 f.

10 : 14 .... The Holy Grail, 551.

11 .... Becket, I, iii, 416.

11 .... In Memoriam, XXXI.

11 : 16 .... The Foresters, I, iii, 102.

11 : 25 .... In Memoriam, XXXII.

11 : 50 .... Queen Mary, IV, iii, 11 f.

12 : 3 .... In Memoriam, XXXII.

12 : 13 .... Enoch Arden, 500-502.

12 : 13 .... Queen Mary, I, v, 61.

13 : 14 .... Becket, I, iv, 222.

13 : 33 f. .... Akbar's Dream, 74.

14 : 6 .... Queen Mary, III, v, 18.

15 : 13 .... Becket, v, ii, 181.

17 : 1 f. .... Queen Mary, IV, iii, 102-104.

18 : 36 .... Becket, v, ii, 10.

19 : 5 .... In Memoriam, LXIX.

19 : 11 .... Becket, II, ii, 257 f.

19 : 11 .... Queen Mary, IV, ii, 94.

19 : 17 .... Sea Dreams, 186 f.

Acts

Romans

1 : 17	Sea Dreams, 153.
1 : 20	The Higher Pantheism.
1 : 21	Morte d'Arthur, 301-304.
2 : 5	Queen Mary, iii, iv, 152.
2 : 15	The Cup, ii, 67.
3 : 6	Queen Mary, iv, iii, 87.
3 : 8	Harold, v, i, 98.
3 : 10	Merlin and Vivien, 50 f.
3 : 23	Becket, v, ii, 307.
4 : 15	Pelleas and Ettarre, 472.
6 : 23	Wages.
6 : 23	The Wreck, 93.
7 : 7	Pelleas and Ettarre, 472.
7 : 18	St. Simeon Stylites, 56 f.
7 : 18, 19, 23	The Two Voices, 301-303.
8 : 16 (Ps. 65 : 2; Acts, 17 : 27)	The Higher Pantheism.
8 : 17	Becket, v, iii, 18.
8 : 24	In Memoriam, Proem.
8 : 28	Sea Dreams, 154 f.
8 : 28	Harold, Show-Day, 1876.
8 : 28	Will Waterproof, 55 f.
8 : 29	Despair, 97.
8 : 34	The Princess, vii, 74.
9 : 27	Queen Mary, iii, i, 168.
10 : 6-8	In Memoriam, cviii.
10 : 17	Queen Mary, iii, i, 157.
12 : 14	Akbar's Dream, 75.
12 : 15	Queen Mary, iv, iii, 10.
12 : 17	Harold, v, i, 99 f.
12 : 19	The Voyage of Maeldune, 120.
12 : 20	Romney's Remorse, 137 f.
13 : 4	Queen Mary, iv, iii, 121.
13 : 8	The Miller's Daughter, 207.
14 : 4	The Grandmother, 95.
14 : 15	The Last Tournament, 62.

TABLE II
(Following Order of Poems)
The Two Voices

The Princess

II, 173..................Acts, 20: 29.
II, 174..................Numbers, 6: 25.
II, 324 f.................1 Kings, 10: 1.
II, 328..................1 Kings, 10: 1.
II, 329..................1 Kings, 4: 31.
II, 330 f.................1 Kings, 10: 4 f.
III, 212-214..............Esther, 1: 12.
III, 242-244.............Proverbs, 10: 1.
III, 306.................Genesis, 1: 3.
III, 309 f................1 Corinthians, 13: 12.
IV, 59, 466 f.............Genesis, 11: 9.
IV, 109 f.................Exodus, 1: 14.
IV, 113..................Matthew, 16: 18.
IV, 122.............   .....Exodus, 15: 20.
IV, 207 f.................Apocrypha, Book of Judith.
IV, 292..................Jonah, 4: 6.
IV, 319..................2 Corinthians, 3: 6.
IV, 388..................Luke, 21: 18.
IV, 484..................Acts, 7: 59 f.
V, 376...................1 Corinthians, 5: 6 f.
V, 417...................Exodus, 7-12 (chapters).
V, 444...................Matthew, 5: 22.
V, 500...................Exodus, 15: 20.
V, 500...................Judges, 4.
VI, 16...................Judges, 5: 1.
VI, 17...................Isaiah, 21: 9.
VI, 17...................Revelation, 18: 2.
VI, 17...................Revelation, 14: 8.
VI, 224..................Genesis, 19: 26.
VII, 74..................Romans, 8: 34.
VII, 188.................Song of Solomon, 2: 15.
VII, 244.................1 Corinthians, 12: 13.
VII, 312.................John, 9: 6.
VII, 277.................Genesis, 2: 8.
Conclusion 115...........Nehemiah, 9: 6.

In Memoriam

LXXXVII ....2 Corinthians, 6 : 16.
LXXXVIII ....Genesis, 2 : 8.
XCV ....Isaiah, 28 : 13.
XCVI ....Genesis, 32 : 24-29.
XCVI ....Exodus, 32 : 1-4.
CIII ....Deuteronomy, 2 : 10.
CVI ....Revelation, 20 : 2-4.
CVIII ....Romans, 10 : 6-8.
CXIV ....Proverbs, 9 : 1.
CXX ....1 Corinthians, 15 : 32.
CXXIV (cf. XCVI).......Genesis, 32 : 29.
CXXXI ....1 Corinthians, 10 : 4.
CXXXI ....1 John, 2 : 17.
CXXXI ....Isaiah, 29 : 4.
CXXXI ....Mark, 16 : 20.
CXXXI ....1 Corinthians, 3 : 9.
CXXXI ....Philippians, 2 : 13.
CXXXI ....Genesis, 2 : 8.
CXXXI ....Luke, 23 : 43.
CXXXI ....Isaiah, 52 : 8.
CXXXI ....1 Corinthians, 15 : 24, 28.

Maud

I, i, 21...................Malachi, 2 : 2.
I, i, 23...................1 John, 3 : 12.
I, i, 31...................Job, 41 : 24.
I, i, 31...................Isaiah, 50 : 7.
I, i, 32...................Genesis, 3 : 19.
I, i, 33, 36...............Micah, 4 : 4.
I, i, 35...................Psalms, 116 : 11.
I, i, 45...................Matthew, 6 : 24.
I, i, 46...................Matthew, 6 : 24.
I, ii, 78..................Matthew, 5 : 13.
I, iv, 143.................Song of Solomon, 4 : 16.
I, iv, 152.................2 Timothy, 3 : 13.
I, vi, 268.................Ezekiel, 11 : 19.

I, x, 396 f................Ephesians, 4:22, 24.
I, xiii, 485................Leviticus, 16:21.
I, xviii, 610................Revelation, 21:21.
I, xviii, 613-616............Psalms, 104:16.
I, xviii, 614................Song of Solomon, 4:16.
I, xviii, 625 ff.............Genesis, 2:8.
I, xviii, 625 ff.............Genesis, 3:18.
II, i, 8....................Genesis, 2:8.
II, i, 34..................Genesis, 4:10, 11.
II, ii, 95, 96...............Genesis, 4:23.
II, iii, 132, 136............Ezekiel, 11:19.
II, v, 285-288.............Luke, 12:3.

CHAPTER I

THE PERIOD OF SIMPLICITY

The term " Period of Simplicity," here employed to designate the first stage in Tennyson's use of Scripture, may perhaps best be understood by a brief survey of its several characteristics. (1) First and foremost the Period of Simplicity is the period of the single passage. This fact is that which most clearly and sharply distinguishes it from the other periods. Each passage of Scripture is cited singly. It is not combined with other passages into a complex unity but stands by itself in literary isolation. (2) In the second place there is no twisting or distorting of the scripture wording. Each passage is used with faithful adherence to its natural, normal, intrinsic meaning in the Bible-text itself. The scripture wording is, indeed, often amplified, vivified, and creatively renewed, but the poetical version of it gives a faithful reflection of the literal biblical meaning, and furnishes, as it were, a poetical exegesis or exposition of it. In later periods Tennyson will take a biblical phrase like " Sons of God and daughters of men " and change it to " Sons of men and daughters of God " (*Aylmer's Field,* 44, 45; *Genesis,* VI, 2), or he will take a Hebrew parallelism like "bone of my bones and flesh of my flesh " and change it to "Flesh of my flesh was gone, but bone of my bone was left " (*Rizpah,* 51; *Genesis,* II, 23). Such " playing upside down with Holy Writ " (cf. *Foresters,* III, 103) is found in abundant examples in the later periods but is conspicuously absent from this first period where the use is simple, direct, literal. (3) In the third place Scripture in this period is sometimes used as a scenic background or stage-setting for the poem in which it appears. Just as the weather and the seasons form a background of nature in keeping with the story in all the *Idylls of the King,* so in this period a biblical scene or picture is occasionally used as a background in keeping with the poem in which it is placed.

(4) In the fourth place, and much more striking than the use of Scripture as a scenic background, is the use of Scripture containing the same thought or theme as the dominant thought or theme of the poem in which it appears. In this case the Scripture furnishes, as it were, the key-note to an understanding of the poem. (5) In the fifth place, Scripture is employed to make a simple simile as contrasted with a compound metaphor, an allegory, or a satirical comparison. Scripture is used for purposes of simple, obvious illustration. All symbolic or satirical use of it is reserved for later periods. (6) Lastly, it is only in this first period that we find any extended or elaborated treatment of a biblical passage. The citations in the later periods are as a rule brief and subordinated to a unifying purpose of some sort. It is only in this first period that the poet takes delight in any broad, sympathetic re-creation of a biblical scene or picture for its own sake.

It is not meant that all these elements of simplicity enumerated above appear in each of the poet's uses of Scripture in this early period or appear with equal distinctness. They are, however, sufficiently in evidence to establish very clearly that there was in the earlier period of Tennyson's career a marked simplicity in his employment of biblical citations. The establishment of such a period in his treatment of biblical material is, moreover, suggestive of a corresponding early period and method in his art and mental processes in general. It is hoped that the detailed study of his later methods of handling the Bible will also prove illustrative and illuminative of corresponding stages of his artistic career in general; but all that is contended for at this point is that, just as there was an early period of simplicity in Tennyson's attitude toward the Bible, so there was also a corresponding early period of simplicity in respect of his complete art and craftsmanship.

The principal portions of Scripture used during this first period relate to the portrait of Stephen in *The Two Voices;* the description of the swine in *The Palace of Art;* the picture of the mist in the garden of Eden in *Geraint and Enid;* the sac-

rifice of Jephthah's daughter in *A Dream of Fair Women;* the
portrait of Mary at Lazarus' supper in *In Memoriam;* and the
song of the foolish virgins in *Guinevere.* There is a large
number of other effective citations, but those just mentioned
are the fullest and most characteristic.   The points enumerated
above in the opening paragraph may be distributed roughly as
follows: points (1) and (2) apply to all six of these citations;
point (3) to the passages in *The Palace of Art* and *Geraint and
Enid;* point (4) to all except *The Palace of Art* and Jephthah's daughter; point (5) to all except Jephthah's daughter;
and point (6) to all the passages.   These citations may now be
studied in detail.[1]

The portrait of Stephen in *The Two Voices* may be cited at
the outset in order to make the simplicity of this period immediately clear.   There are, says the poet, calm and disciplined
souls who have at last become

> Like Stephen, an unquenched fire.
> He heeded not reviling tones,
> Nor sold his heart to idle moans,
> Tho' curs'd and scorn'd and bruised with stones;
>
> But looking upward, full of grace,
> He pray'd, and from a happy place
> God's glory smote him on the face.   (219-225)

(1) This is the Stephen of the Sixth and Seventh Chapters
of *Acts.*   No other biblical mention of him is added.   No
lines taken from any other biblical hero's face are worked into
the picture.   Tennyson is adhering to his rule of one passage
at a time.   (2) He is also observing his rule of faithfulness
to the passage chosen.   The portrait of Stephen is true to the
apostolic record.   The details are, indeed, concentrated, unified, and vivified.   The angelic face before the speech, the
vision at its close, and the act of prayer are vividly interwoven.
But it is the Stephen that ordinary readers of the Bible know.
He is not retouched beyond clearest recognition.   (4) Further-

---

[1] For the sake of clearness and convenience the numbered points will be
inserted at their proper places in the discussion of each citation.

more, there is a harmony or identity of thought between the passage chosen and the poem which includes it. The poem is a sermon of which Stephen is the text. He is, as it were, the inspired embodiment of the meaning and motif of the whole poem. What else, indeed, is the poem to teach, if it be not to inspire that final trust which makes no moan and heeds no bitter or reviling voice, but endures and achieves because it has a cleared vision of an immortal and over-ruling spirit of love seen in an opened heaven? (5) But the harmony of thought is, after all, essentially simple. There is no use made of allegory, satire, or metaphor as in later periods. Stephen is not the symbol of a power or faculty of the soul. He is not satirized by some bitter skeptic. He is merely the historic scriptural character whom some souls resemble; the passage is used purely for the purpose of simple illustration, and (6) the poet evidently delights in it for its own sake as well as in its connections.

One passage at a time was Tennyson's invariable practice during this period. A further illustration of this fact is found in the repellent picture of swine in *The Palace of Art*.

> O Godlike isolation which art mine,
>   I can but count thee perfect gain,
> What time I watch the darkening droves of swine
>   That range on yonder plain.
>
> In filthy sloughs they roll a prurient skin,
>   They graze and wallow, breed and sleep;
> And oft some brainless devil enters in,
>   And drives them to the deep.   (197-204)

(1) In these lines the only biblical passage before us (*Luke*, VIII, 30-33) relates to the Gadarene swine. There is no admixture from outside verses. In striking contrast to this is the following passage from *Queen Mary* taken from a later period of this study:—

> *Philip.* Ay, Lambeth has ousted Cranmer.
>   It was not meet the heretic swine should live in Lambeth.
> *Mary.* There or anywhere, or at all.
> *Philip.* We have had it swept and garnish'd after him.
> *Pole.* Not for the seven devils to enter in?
> *Philip.* No, for we trust they parted in the swine.
>   (III, ii, 79-84)

Whatever effectiveness these lines may have, it is evident that
in them the poet does not care to retain a single citation of
Scripture in separate distinctness, but, for the sake of kindred imagery, and it may be for other reasons, is willing to
combine and confuse one passage with another. As in *The
Palace of Art* so here there is imagery taken from the story of
the Gadarene swine. But it is combined with other imagery
taken from Jesus' comparison of his generation to the house
to which the exorcised demon returns with seven others (*Matthew,* xii, 43-45). Furthermore, the description is not meant to
be taken simply and literally but constitutes a compound metaphor to which the *dramatis personae* contribute their several
parts. It is just this combining and figurative use of Scripture which is conspicuously absent from the Period of Sim-
picity. The two examples taken together, the one from *The
Palace of Art* and the other from *Queen Mary*—the former as
an example of what Tennyson does in this period and the latter
as an example of what he does not do—make exceptionally
clear the statement that till after his fiftieth year he used
scriptural passages in an isolated and uncombined form.

(3) The passage from *The Palace of Art* also affords an
illustration of the occasional use of the outstanding scripture
element in these earlier poems as a scenic background. Such
a background always serves to enhance and bring out the meaning of the poem just as the weather and the seasons do in the
Idylls of the King. Here is the soul in haughty egoistic isolation looking down upon the contemptible remainder of mankind, now coarse and brutish, and now again filled with the
red fool-fury of the Seine. There at the back of the stage is
the painted scene of a proud, strong man watching the swine
wallow and then with demonic inspiration make their suicidal
rush into the sea. The two pictures are much akin. (5) Yet
it is a very simple and unelaborated likeness. It is, indeed,
satirical in its view of men but there is no satire upon the Scripture itself such as is found, for example, in the later additions
to *Merlin and Vivien.*

A still further and perhaps more striking example of the use
of Scripture as a scenic background is that found in *Geraint and
Enid*. The description of Eden is as follows:

> And never yet, since high in Paradise
> O'er the four rivers the first roses blew,
> Came purer pleasure unto mortal kind
> Than lived thro' her who in that perilous hour
> Put hand to hand beneath her husband's heart
> And felt him hers again. She did not weep,
> But o'er her meek eyes came a happy mist
> Like that which kept the heart of Eden green
> Before the useful trouble of the rain.
>
> (762-770)

(3) The predominant feature of this passage is undoubt-
edly its scenic quality. The picture of Eden furnishes an
appropriate scenic background for the story that is being told,
just as the weather and the seasons do in the same idyll. It
is the time of mowers and mowing. The sun blazes on the
turning scythe. The full summer-time is in tune with the ripe
wedded love of Geraint and Enid and with the ripening strength
of the Round Table. The reference to Eden is a similarly appropriate piece of stage-scenery. (4) But there is also a harmony of thought or correspondence of idea between the Bible-
passage and that of the poem. The picture, or suggested picture, of wedded Eden happiness corresponds with the ripe married happiness of Geraint and Enid. There is ideal happiness
in each case. (5) The harmony of thought is, however, essentially simple and obvious. The happiness of Enid with Geraint was like the happiness of Eve with Adam in the Garden.
The passage is quoted by Tennyson merely for the purpose of
simple illustration. There is no allegory here, much less any
satire as in his biblical passages which appear in subsequent
periods. The rivers are rivers, the roses are roses, the mist is
a mist, and the rain is a rain. They are not symbols of human
life, or of love, of doubt or of divine grace. The comparison is
a simile, and the simile is simple in its precision. The mist in
Enid's eyes is like the mist in Eden. A simile is made up of
two halves: the thing and the thing it is like. The thing it is

like is in this case to be taken simply and literally. · In this early period Tennyson's biblical figures were essentially similes. It is hardly necessary to call attention to the fact that (1) the citation is single.   Just the one passage in *Genesis* is used. There is no admixture of outside verses.   (2) Here also is exemplified fidelity to the natural, primary meaning of the biblical text.   The re-creation is finely imagined and skillfully wrought, but there is no twisting or distorting of the wording or meaning of the Bible-text.   (6) Lastly this passe in *Geraint and Enid* gives a somewhat extended or elaborate picture of a Bible-scene and thus affords an illustration of all six of the points enumerated above as characteristic of this early period.

(6) A more striking example, however, than this from *Geraint and Enid* of the extended and elaborated treatment of a Bible-scene is to be found in the Song of Jephthah's daughter in *A Dream of Fair Women*.   (1) Here, too, it may be parenthetically said, the poet still adheres to his rule of one passage at a time, which in this case is a few verses from the eleventh chapter of *Judges*.   The clear bird-voice of Jephthah's daughter sings:

> The torrent brooks of hallow'd Israel
>   From craggy hollows pouring, late and soon,
> Sound all night long, in falling thro' the dell,
>   Far-heard beneath the moon.
>
> The balmy moon of blessed Israel
>   Floods all the deep-blue gloom with beams divine;
> All night the splinter'd crags that wall the dell
>   With spires of silver shine.
>
> (181-188)
>
> Leaving the olive-gardens far below,
>   Leaving the promise of my bridal bower,
> The valleys of grape-loaded vines that glow
>   Beneath the battled tower.
>
> The light white cloud swam over us.   Anon
>   We heard the lion roaring from his den;
> We saw the large white stars rise one by one,
>   Or, from the darken'd glen,
>
> Saw God divide the night with flying flame,
>   And thunder on the everlasting hills.   (217-226)

(2) The whole song, moreover, is written with simplest fidelity to the scriptural story. The poet rearranges the verses, to be sure, for the sake of artistic effect and makes the mountain song come first. He also gives us imaginative amplifications, but there is no twisting or turning of the biblical wording or meaning. The Bible gives the one word "mountains." Tennyson makes it scenic. The noise of the mountain torrent is heard and the moon-silvered crags are seen towering above the vine-yard village below. The wild beast roars and the mountain-storm gathers and breaks. The Bible tells of "two months." Tennyson expresses this by speaking of one moon and one "when the next moon was rolled into the sky." But however rich and ringing he may make his description, he does it in faithful accord with the biblical wording and story. His scenery is such as might be used in a geography of Palestine. The entire song of the poet, though imaginative, is faithful, conscientious exegesis of the biblical narrative.

In other stanzas the oath of Jephthah is denounced, the maiden mourns her childless life, and gathers strength to make her death seem a beautiful thing. Still in agreement with the original passage (*Judges,* xi, 32 f.), she rises into a religious fervor that weaves even the geographic names into high music for the glory of God.

> 'Moreover it is written that my race
>   Hew'd Ammon, hip and thigh, from Aroer
> On Arnon unto Minneth.' Here her face
>   Glow'd, as I look'd at her.
>
> She lock'd her lips; she left me where I stood:
>   'Glory to God,' she sang, and past afar,
> Thridding the sombre boskage of the wood,
>   Toward the morning-star.   (237-244)

In Memoriam contains many references to Scripture that are all simple and direct in the sense already explained. The best known is, perhaps, the following:

> And so the Word had breath, and wrought
>   With human hands the creed of creeds
>   In loveliness of perfect deeds,
> More strong than all poetic thought.   (xxxvi)

Other examples are: the sinless years that breathed beneath the Syrian blue (LII), the hope that reaches behind the veil (LVI), the shining hand of Him that died in Holy Land (LXXXIV), and the table-scene with the portrait of Mary, which may be especially and fully quoted as follows:

> When Lazarus left his charnel-cave,
>   And home to Mary's house return'd,
>   Was this demanded—if he yearn'd
> To hear her weeping by his grave?
>
> 'Where wert thou, brother, those four days?'
>   There lives no record of reply,
>   Which telling what it is to die
> Had surely added praise to praise.
>
> From every house the neighbors met,
>   The streets were fill'd with joyful sound,
>   A solemn gladness even crown'd
> The purple brows of Olivet.
>
> Behold a man raised up by Christ!
>   The rest remaineth unreveal'd;
>   He told it not, or something seal'd
> The lips of that Evangelist.
>
> Her eyes are homes of silent prayer,
>   Nor other thought her mind admits
>   But, he was dead, and there he sits,
> And He that brought him back is there.
>
> Then one deep love doth supersede
>   All other, when her ardent gaze
>   Roves from the living brother's face,
> And rests upon the Life indeed.
>
> All subtle thought, all curious fears,
>   Borne down by gladness so complete,
>   She bows, she bathes the Saviour's feet
> With costly spikenard and with tears.
>
>   (XXXI, XXXII)

(1) These lines might be printed in parallel columns with the corresponding verses in the twelfth chapter of *John*. The poem makes use of no other scripture material. Certainly the " tears " do not come from the seventh of *Luke*. Mary is not a " sinner." Here also one passage at a time marks Tenny-

son's attitude of mind toward Scripture. (2) In addition he is also faithful to the natural and literal sense of the fourth evangelist. There is no warping of biblical words or phrases. Tennyson, to be sure, re-conceives the picture in his own imaginative way and adds new and vivifying details, but he does so in agreement with the biblical narrative. There is no wrenching or distorting of its wording or meaning and the poetical exposition is, after all, but a faithful exegesis of the Bible-text.

(4) Once more, there is scarcely any other passage in the whole Bible that could have furnished such a sympathetic atmosphere or such a harmony of thought; for there is no other incident that combines sickness, death, entombment, resurrection, and restoration to home-life and table-talk. It is an instance of the complete re-union of souls in and with Christ, after the death of one of them who was greatly beloved. What else is the long-drawn desire that runs through this whole series of a hundred and thirty-one scientific and psychological "poems"? It is the gladness of immortality crowning nature and human intercourse. It is the resurrection and the life. Even the mystery and the questioning that pervade the whole *In Memoriam* are not absent from the scriptural picture of the faith. It is the entire poem, as it were, that selects the scripture citation. The two convey essentially the same general thought. The scripture passage, in a sense, affords a key-note to an understanding of the poem. (5) But again the point of simplicity needs to be insisted on. The biblical illustration is essentially simple and obvious. It serves as a kind of simile or picture-half of a simile; but there is no allegory, no metaphor, no abstract speculation, no satire. The portrayal, tho discriminatingly profound, is yet simple. It may also be noted in passing that the citation in question, in addition to serving as an illustration of the underlying thought of the entire poem, also incidentally serves to enhance and bring out the special principles set forth in the stanzas immediately following in the poem. But in either case the nature of the scripture illustration is that of plain, obvious simile as contrasted with involved, allegorical comparison.

3

(6) In conclusion, this passage is also, perhaps, the finest example in the period (unless possibly the song of Jephthah's daughter be excepted) of an extended and elaborated treatment of a Bible-passage.   The uses of Scripture in the later periods are all brief and incidental to some unifying purpose.   This is perhaps the best example of that full, imaginative entrance into scripture scene and story and of that extended, detailed, poetical re-creation of it for its own sake which characterize this period and do not reappear in any subsequent one.

One of the earliest Idylls, *Guinevere,* furnishes a closing example of the qualities of Tennyson's Period of Simplicity. In the night Arthur has found the sinful queen in the abbey. His figure is spiritual and almost weird.   He has paused before Guinevere in the darkness.   She has hidden her face.

> Then came silence, then a voice,
> Monotonous and hollow like a ghost's
> Denouncing judgment.
>
> (416-418)

This at once recalls the highly-wrought passage in *Job* iv, 15, 16, " A spirit passed before my face . . . It stood still . . . . . There was silence and I heard a voice."   The night, the weirdness, the silence, and the arraignment of human frailty that follows in both cases make the allusion highly effective.   The effect, however, is direct and simple.   (1) The scripture basis is that of the vision in *Job* alone.   No other biblical allusion is added, and the passage envelops the meeting of Arthur and the queen like a presence to be felt rather than described.

Another scripture passage furnishes, however, a more definite and complete harmonious background than this for the subjective feeling that pervades the whole idyll.   It is in the little maid's song of the Foolish Virgins.   The motif of *Guinevere* is " Too Late."   The queen's parting with Lancelot had come too late; her repentance was too late; when from the court she fled through the night, she

> Heard the spirits of the waste and weald
> Moan as she fled, or thought she heard them moan.
> And in herself she moan'd, ' Too late, too late! '
>
> (128-130)

After Arthur had gone the voice of her last longing was the same

> Still hoping, fearing 'Is it yet too late'?

(685)

Now, the song of the little maid is a peculiarly effective scriptural background for this sense of sad and irreparable ruin.

> Late, late, so late! and dark the night and chill!
> Late, late, so late! but we can enter still.
> Too late, too late! ye cannot enter now.
>
> No light had we; for that we do repent,
> And learning this, the bridegroom will relent.
> Too late, too late! ye cannot enter now.
>
> No light! so late! and dark and chill the night!
> O, let us in that we may find the light!
> Too late, too late! ye cannot enter now.
>
> Have we not heard the bridegroom is so sweet?
> O, let us in, tho' late, to kiss his feet!
> No, no, too late! ye cannot enter now.

(166-177)

Tennyson imparts the pathetic feeling of this song to the whole abbey as well as to the queen by saying that the nuns had taught the exquisite stanzas to the little maid. To summarize briefly: (1) it is clear that only one portion of one parable is used; (2) that the song is faithful to the evangelist's meaning; (4) that the scripture background it affords is natural and unaffected; that the harmony of thought is a simple one—being in this instance the idea of irreparableness; and (5) that there is no satire at the expense of Scripture, and no allegorizing of its words, but only a simple re-creating from it of a song of which the burden is the burden of the poet's story.

When the four idylls of 1859 were published, two thirds of Tennyson's poetic production was still in the future. But that two-thirds was to contain among its many songs no successor to those of Jephthah's daughter and the little maid. Nothing in Eden was to be described in the simple manner of the passage in *Geraint and Enid*. It is in vain to search for any scripture portrait like that of Stephen or Mary. It is not within the

province of this study to discuss the causes in the poet's mind
or in his age that brought the period of simplicity to its
close.   The matter may perhaps be referable to a theory of the
gradual and cautious development of Tennyson's mind.   Many
poets start out with complexity and achieve simplicity only
after years of toil and effort.   Tennyson's evolution from simplicity into complexity is perhaps merely a natural result of
his self-controlled disposition, of his temperamental restraint,
and of his increasing richness and variety of mental equipment.
But whatever the cause of the cessation in Tennyson's case, it
involved a loss to the laureate's readers.   The re-creating of
the old Bible-scenes was well worth while.   The delight they
still afford is the proof.   Whatever pleasure the scripture
mosaics of the next period may give and whatever spiciness
there may be in the satirical uses that come still later, the
paintings of the days of simplicity will nevertheless be missed.
The subsequent different handling of biblical material will
yield combinations and polarizations full of beauty and power.
Many readers, however, would gladly give up the best of them to
hear the little maid sing another parable, or see another Mary
whose eyes were homes of silent prayer.

CHAPTER II

THE PERIOD OF COMBINATION

The Second period in Tennyson's use of Scripture may be defined as the period of combination. The period of the single passage has given way to the period of combined passages, taken in many cases from widely separated chapters. It exhibits the following characteristics: (1) the use of each separate scriptural passage is allusive and suggestive, as distinguished from the extended and elaborated uses of the first period; (2) several brief citations or allusions are closely connected together to form a single unified poetic passage; (3) the unity of each combination proceeds from some non-scriptural thought, emotion, or purpose which, working upon the scripture material, coördinates or organizes the separate references; (4) these artistic combinations are based upon, and made possible by, an attitude toward Scripture in general that is freer than that of the first period; (5) this period is marked off from succeeding periods by two interesting negative facts, (a) the presence of scriptureless allegory, (b) the reverent use of Scripture for a satirical purpose.

1. In this period no scripture citation is wrought out into the stanzas of an extended song or into the features of a full and living portrait. Even where the use is essentially the same in principle, the scripture allusion is never expanded or pictured out, as in the first period. In *Sea Dreams* the heated pulpiteer casts Babylon, like a great stone, into the sea. The noise of the fall becomes a part of the vision in the city clerk's dream. But however artistic the employment of the citation, it is simply allusive. In *Enoch Arden* Annie tells her intuition to Enoch, " I shall look upon your face no more." This is evidently meant to suggest the seashore sorrow of Paul's friends because they should " behold his face no more." [1]

[1] *Acts*, xx, 38.

Tennyson might have wrought out this beautiful allusion in the extended manner of the first period. But he gives only the one scripture phrase, which he puts into the mouth of Annie. It suggests the picture in *Acts,* but does not paint it. In *Aylmer's Field* Edith is " pale as the Jephtha's daughter." The words are finely prophetic of her sacrifice to a parent's pride. The allusion seems to invite a full artistic portrait like that of Mary in *In Memoriam.* But, again, Tennyson does not paint it. The brief words quoted above are all that he actually gives. Such condensed allusions as these may now have seemed to Tennyson more artistic and effective than the earlier and fuller elaborations. But the fact that extended portrayal is repressed even in such inviting instances as these emphasizes the change of artistic method which now appears. The second period makes its references to Scripture merely allusive, because only brief allusions lend themselves readily to combination with others; and combination is the new and dominant note of this period.

2. The combinations in this period are to be clearly distinguished from mere aggregations of texts and from scriptural chains. In the *Supposed Confessions* there is a long series of scripture quotations. There is another in *St. Simeon Stylites.* These aggregations are not, however, anticipations of the method of artistic combination. There is perhaps a score of scripture references in each of these poems. But no two or more of them are directly united into one image, or, taken together, express a single thought, purpose, or emotion. The score of citations expresses a corresponding score of separate mental conceptions.

3. The new method appeared with the *Enoch Arden* volume in 1864. Enoch is trying to comfort Annie:

> Cast all your cares on God; that anchor holds.
> Is He not yonder in those uttermost
> Parts of the morning? If I flee to these,
> Can I go from Him? and the sea is His,
> The sea is His; He made it.   (222-226)

Each phrase in this quotation is from the King James Version. The passages cited are as far apart as the First Epistle of Peter,

THE
UNIVERSITY OF WINNIPEG
PORTAGE & BALMORAL
WINNIPEG 2, MAN.
CANADA
DISCARDED

the Epistle to the Hebrews, and Psalms One-Hundred-Thirty-nine and Ninety-five. Yet they are perfectly unified by the single idea of comfort that the God who made the sea cares for the sea-faring man. The artistic unity is so perfect that it makes the reader forget how widely the component phrases and allusions are separated from one another in the Bible. Such unifying of biblical suggestions marks a new method of handling scripture material. There is none of it in the first period.

Another method of combination consists of a series of allusions expressing various degrees of a single quality or characteristic and coming to a climax. It is to be noted that this method, if it may be called a method, is an application to scripture material of the frequent artistic device of anaphora. Two instances out of many may be given here. Galahad reaches at last a state of soul in which he always sees the Holy Grail. It is

> Fainter by day, but always in the night
> Blood-red, and sliding down the blackened marsh
> Blood-red, and on the naked mountain-top
> Blood-red, and in the sleeping mere below
> Blood-red.
>
> *(Holy Grail, 472-476)*

Again, the invocation of love upon Victoria:

> May all love,
> His love, unseen but felt, o'ershadow thee,
> The love of all thy sons encompass thee,
> The love of all thy daughters cherish thee,
> The love of all thy people comfort thee,
> Till God's love set thee at his side again.
>
> *(Dedication, 48-53)*

It is in a similar manner that Tennyson uses scripture material in *Aylmer's Field*. Edith is

> Fairer than Rachel by the palmy well,
> Fairer than Ruth among the fields of corn,
> Fair as the angel that said " Hail."
>
> *(679-681)*

The anaphora is made effective by the three suggestive allusions to Scripture. Still another style of combination is seen in

the swindling mine-promoter's talk in *Sea Dreams*.   Here the
scripture quotations are unified into a hypocritical appeal for
confidence.

> When the great Books—see Daniel seven and ten—
> Were open'd, I should find he meant me well;
>
> . . . .
>
>   " My dearest friend,
> Have faith, have faith! We live by faith," said he;
> ' And all things work together for the good
> Of those '—it makes me sick to quote him.
>
>   (148-155)

This, then, is Tennyson's new method with Scripture as
seen in the second period. The contrast with the first period
is clear. In that period each scripture passage was valued for
its independent worth. It was not subordinated to the larger
purposes of any combination. It was a single gem cut and
polished and set in the surrounding non-scriptural matter.
In this new period several scriptural gems are set together
so as to form a single artistic piece of jewelry. In the first
period the unity of each scripture passage was to be found in
itself. It was inherent. In the characteristic passages of the
second period the citations have no unity of their own. They
are wrought into a unity thru the agency of some non-scriptural
thought or purpose which, working upon them in connection
with other scriptural references, organizes or coördinates the
whole into one idea.

It is also to be observed that in this second period, as well
as in the first, Tennyson uses each separate scripture passage
without mutilation or serious alteration. Each citation is taken
at its face value. The poet is still faithful to the natural and
ordinary meaning of Scripture. The passages are used for
their implications, used as side-lights, used for all kinds of suggestive coloring; but the implications and suggestions are
never essentially untrue to the natural meanings of the biblical
passages. Even the swindling mine-promoter in *Sea Dreams*
uses the Bible just as an honest Christian *might* have done.
This is not true, as will be seen in the following chapters, of
the Allegorical and Satirical Periods.

4. This period, moreover, marks a progress in the freedom of Tennyson's art. In the first period each scripture passage was regarded as an inviolable shrine. It might be restored, beautified, or illuminated. But there was, as has already been implied, no thought of using it along with other passages as mere building-material. The hand of a builder that treats old buildings as quarries for new ones is intrinsically much more free than the hand that merely restores and beautifies. In the period of simplicity the natural sense and meaning of the Scripture used controlled the ideas connected with it; but in this second stage the connected ideas control the use of the Scripture. It may become a mere fetish and may mislead. In *Enoch Arden* thought-transference is a faithful guide, whereas the use of the Bible results in a wrong impression. Annie says to Philip, " Enoch lives. That is borne in upon me." When at last she married Philip,

> A footstep seem'd to fall beside her path,
> She knew not whence; a whisper on her ear,
> She knew not what. (510-512)

She was afraid to enter her own house. The bells had rung merrily when Annie and Philip were wedded, and far away upon his lone island Enoch heard his parish bells peal faintly but merrily and started up shuddering.[2] The very night, in fact the very moment, that Edith died, Leolin, as the story is told in *Aylmer's Field,* shrieked her name in his sleep.[3] Thus Tennyson during this second period appears to have been strongly under the influence of the idea of thought-transference. He asked the question:

> Star to star vibrates light; may soul to soul
> Strike through a finer element of her own?
> So,—from afar,—touch as at once? (578-580)

If Annie had obeyed this true and faithful instinct she would have delayed her marriage to Philip, and Enoch on his return would have been spared his agony; but she consulted her Bible.

---

[2] Cf. 507 ff. and 609 ff.   [3] 576-592.

It is true she used it as a fetish; she sprang up in the night, flung it open, put her finger on the page at random, and read, "Under the palm-tree." She closed the book, slept, and dreamed of Enoch sitting under a palm. He must be in heaven, she thought, where the palms are. So she married Philip. The fact that Tennyson could describe so finely the superstitious use of the Bible by Annie is suggestive. The simple and religious woman to whom the portrait of Mary in *In Memoriam* is likened stands in strong contrast to the biblically misled but also simple and religious wife of Enoch. Annie's use of the Bible may be realistic, but in his first period Tennyson would scarcely have felt free or have had the heart to draw the portrait. Yet for the artistic combination of small portions of Scripture into the larger unities of the period of combination some such larger liberty of feeling in regard to the biblical literature as a whole seems naturally required.

5(*a*). The period of combination is marked off from the later periods by two interesting facts. In a succeeding period Scripture is used for the purposes of allegory. No such use is made in the present period. But this is not because the period contains no allegory. In *Sea-Dreams* there is a fine allegorical picture of a mystic, incoming tide charged with destruction and with music. Critics interpret it antithetically. For Brooke it is the great incoming deep of eternal love destroying the impermanent forms of religion over which men quarrel.[5] Van Dyke thinks it is the rising tide of doubt threatening to undermine and overwhelm the beliefs of the past.[6] This allegory, tho relating to religious truth and naturally allied to Scripture, is not expressed in biblical language or with the help of biblical allusions. This fact shows that in this second period Tennyson had not yet permitted himself to use biblical language for purposes of allegory.

(*b*). The other fact referred to is that, altho this period con-

---

[5] Stopford Brooke, *Tennyson: His Art and Relation to Modern Times*, pp. 42 f.

[6] Henry Van Dyke, *The Gospel for an Age of Doubt*, pp. 20 f.

tains no biblical satire, the satiric mood is not absent. In
Sea Dreams the mine-promoter's use of Scripture gives the
effect of " measureless satire." In Averill's sermon in *Aylmer's
Field* allusions to Scripture are poured forth in a torrent of
molten scorn; but there is no irreverent use in all this satire.
Not a line of it is at the expense of Scripture. In the satirical
period Tennyson constructs his most effective satire by putting
blasphemous uses of sacred words into the mouths of bad characters. The fact that the satire of this present period is in this
respect reverent, or supposedly reverent, is an additional proof
that it is clearly separate from the period of satire as well as
from the period of allegory, so far as this distinction relates to
the use of biblical material.

CHAPTER III

The Period of Allegorizing

By the allegorizing period is meant, in this study, not Tennyson's allegorizing years in general, but the time when he applied his allegorizing powers to biblical material. Allegory without Scripture appears, as already noted, in the second period, the period of Scripture Combination. But the allegorizing use of Scripture does not appear till the third or Allegorizing Period, as designated in this study. This delayed application represents a general principle governing Tennyson's artistic use, which is his only use, of the biblical material. All the stages of his use of the Bible run parallel to similar stages in his use of other material. But the scripture line of the parallel begins further on than the general line. Each separate method of using the Bible has already been preceded by the same method of using other matter. In other words, the application of an artistic method to scripture material marks the "bloom-time" or culminating strength of that method. This general statement is illustrated and confirmed by the following facts. When Tennyson wrote the *Morte d'Arthur* in 1842, he followed the Chronicler's old romance faithfully and breathed its very atmosphere. Seventeen years later he published four complete idylls. But in these he remoulded and essentially altered the old legends. Critics complain of the changes. Tennyson's Enid, they say, as compared with the Chronicler's, is too patient. Geraint's jealousy does not exhibit enough madness to excuse his meanness. He is lost in a vanity and suspicion *of which there is nothing in the original story.* Again, in Tennyson, Vivien the woman is said to be confused with Vivien as Luxuria.[1] This confusion does not, of course, appear in the Chronicles themselves. Whether just or unjust,

---

[1] Stopford Brooke, *op. cit.*, 283 f., 306.

these criticisms serve to show the freedom with which Tennyson altered the original legends. But in this very period of free alteration of legends, Tennyson in his use of Scripture follows the biblical text and communicates its atmosphere as faithfully as, back in 1842, in the *Morte d'Arthur* he followed the old Chronicles. So far as handling the Bible is concerned, he is still in the Period of Simplicity. The presence of scriptureless allegory in the Period of Combination was thus preceded by the analogous presence of free alteration of legends in company with unaltered Scripture in the Period of Simplicity. A third fact may now be recalled, that in the period of allegorizing there is much satire discoverable. However, just as has been observed of the period of combination, there is no satire at the expense of Scripture; for Tennyson has not yet fully developed his satirical art or settled into his satirical mood.

The general fact that Tennyson does not apply an artistic method to Scripture till it has become mature has considerable value for the student of Tennyson's art as seen in the *Idylls* as well as elsewhere. For comparatively few readers are thoroly familiar with the Arthurian Chronicles. Familiarity with material is prerequisite to a clear understanding of its manipulation. The Bible, however, does lie upon the table and its material is familiar, or at least easily accessible. Knowledge of how the artist uses the biblical matter furnishes a clue and guide for studying his use of other matter which is less familiar. It serves also as a kind of headline locating the period to which a poem or passage belongs. Tennyson, moreover, was constantly going back to poems written many years before in order to revise, rearrange, or augment them. These alterations are made, as a rule, according to the prevailing artistic mood of the poet at the time of making them. The same poem may thus combine different artistic methods in a way that confuses the really clear order of the poet's artistic development. But the way Scripture is used in making such changes often reveals at a glance the real date of the deft and otherwise homogeneous additions, and enables us to assign the different sections to their chronological place in the poet's artistic development. The foregoing remarks are fitting in connection with the allegorical division of this study because the *Idylls* as now published are Tennyson's great allegory. Yet they contain examples of all four methods of using Scripture: the simple, the combining, the allegorical, and the satirical.

The Allegorical Period exhibits the following characteristics: (1) The general freedom of attitude toward Scripture observed in the second period develops into a definite and constructive force. (2) Scriptural statements and images and their obvious meanings are freely altered, mixed with legendary matter, and put on an artistic level with it. (3) The scripture citations are often indefinite and doubtful. (4) There is no satirical or scornful use of Scripture. (5) The process or method by which an allegory is made is incidentally shown. (6) The allegorical period marks a distinct advance in Tennyson's artistic power.

1. In his great central work on the *Idylls,* Tennyson's intellectual power is devoted to allegorizing. This statement applies not only to the four new idylls published in 1869 viz: *The Coming of Arthur, The Holy Grail, Pelleas and Ettarre,* and *The Passing of Arthur,* but also to the many alterations and additions made in those previously published,[2] as well as, of course, to those published at later dates. Now it is of the very nature of allegory to favor a freely constructive hand. For the story constructed need not have any very precise verisimi-

---

[2] An example of the allegorical character of the additions which, under the inspiration of his allegorical period, Tennyson made in earlier idylls, may be found in *Merlin and Vivien.* In the original idyll he had already told of Merlin's deep melancholy. He now sees that the vagueness of such a mood affords a fine opportunity for introducing hidden and mystic meanings. Accordingly, he goes back to that idyll and inserts the following lines which did not appear at all in the earlier printing.

> He walk'd with dreams and darkness, and he found
> A doom that ever poised itself to fall,
> An ever-moaning battle in the mist,
> World-war of dying flesh against the life,
> Death in all life and lying in all love,
> The meanest having power upon the highest,
> And the high purpose broken by the worm.
>
> *Merlin and Vivien,* 188-194.

litude. Often it cannot, for it must be flexible to the behests of the secret meanings it carries and must often alter its natural course in accordance with inner requirements. In other words, the story, or scene, or statements which the allegorist uses must often be altered or even transformed in order to meet his specific purposes. By contrast with Tennyson's *Idylls* Bunyan's *Pilgrim's Progress* makes this fact instructively clear. The natural scenery in *Pilgrim's Progress* is not altogether such as we see in the visible world. Bunyan has used freedom in creating it. The story, if taken literally, has many improbabilities. On the other hand, it does use the Bible with faithfulness to its plain and ordinary meanings and statements. This is because Bunyan's allegorical purpose is the same as the purpose of the Bible. He alters his other material freely. But he need not and must not alter his Bible. The Bible, or Christian experience put in a biblical way, is, in fact, Bunyan's motif, his secret allegorical meaning to which his story must be freely adapted and for which it must be freely created. The only allegories the Bible contains are like that in the fifth chapter of *Isaiah* concerning the relation of God to Israel, or that in the fifteenth of *John* concerning the relation of Christ to his disciples. It is these same relations with which Bunyan deals. Tennyson's allegory on the other hand is psychological. Arthur is the rational soul. Merlin is intellectual power. Guinevere is the heart. The knights of the round table are the powers and faculties of the soul. The three queens are faith, hope, and love. The Lady of the Lake is the Church.[3] For such an allegory the Bible cannot furnish the motif as it did for Bunyan, but only the material or vehicle to be freely altered and adapted to the non-biblical purpose. This freedom in altering the biblical matter is a characteristic mark of Tennyson's Allegorical Period.

2. The free alteration of scripture ideas and images and the mixture of legendary with scriptural matter appear in many

[3] Cf. Stopford Brooke, *Tennyson: His Art and Relation to Modern Times*, 260.

passages. *The Holy Grail* gives the following account of the cup of the Lord's Supper: [4]

> The cup, the cup itself, from which our Lord
> Drank at the last sad supper with his own.
> This, from the blessed land of Aromat—
> After the day of darkness, when the dead
> Went wandering o'er Moriah—the good saint
> Arimathaean Joseph, journeying brought
> To Glastonbury, where the winter thorn
> Blossoms at Christmas, mindful of our Lord.
> And there awhile it bode; and if a man
> Could touch or see it, he was heal'd at once,
> By faith, of all his ills. But then the times
> Grew to such evil that the holy cup
> Was caught away to heaven, and disappeared.
>
> (46-58)

Jesus did perhaps drink of the cup which he gave to his disciples. There was darkness over the land for three hours. Many bodies of the saints arose and entered the Holy City and appeared unto many, tho the evangelists do not speak of them as "wandering" or give the impression of a vague walking about in any particular part of Jerusalem. Entirely legendary also are the transportation, appearance, and disappearance of the cup, the blossoming of the winter thorn at Christmas, the healing touch, and the rapture of the cup to heaven. Yet all these legendary features are blended into the story so as to become integral parts of it and are put upon an artistic level with the scriptural items. There was no such levelling blending of Bible and legend anywhere in Tennyson's previous work.

In another passage from the same idyll there is a clear enough allusion to the New Jerusalem and its gates of pearl:

> I saw the spiritual city and all her spires
> And gateways in a glory like one pearl—
> No larger, tho' the goal of all the saints—
> Strike from the sea.
>
> (526-529)

But how changed is the mystic city. Each of the twelve gates in the scripture account is made from a single colossal pearl

---

[4] Cf. *Matthew*, XXVI, 27-29; XXVII, 45, 52, 53, 57.

(*Rev.* xxi, 21) ; in the idyll the whole city, including the gateways, is of the size of one ordinary pearl. This is because the presence and glory of God are in the Holy Cup and the glory must fill the city. Spiritual things, moreover, have no dimensions for Tennyson. The allegory requires the extreme contraction of the size of the scriptural city, and the contraction is, therefore, unhesitatingly and strikingly made.

The little sub-allegory of Humility which the Holy Hermit preaches to Percivale affords an example of intricate and interwoven alterations of scripture language and imagery:

> O son, thou hast not true humility,
> The highest virtue, mother of them all;
> For when the Lord of all things made Himself
> Naked of Glory for his mortal change,
> ' Take thou my robe,' she said, ' for all is thine,'
> And all her form shone forth with sudden light
> So that the angels were amazed, and she
> Follow'd Him down, and like a flying star
> Led on the gray-hair'd wisdom of the east.
>
> (445-453)

Here is easily recognized the language of *1 Peter,* v, 5, " Be clothed with humility " ; of *Philippians,* ii, 5-7, the classical passage for the kenosis or humiliation of Christ; of *Matthew,* xvii, 2, describing the transfiguration; and of *Matthew,* ii, 9, describing the star in the East. But Humility is the allegorical lady herself and therefore she cannot be the robe, but must bestow it even upon the Christ. He must put it on, and therefore does not make himself " of no reputation " or " empty " himself, but " makes himself naked." The star can no longer lead the Magi. Humility herself must do that, and so she takes the likeness of a flying star. It is she, moreover, who, in order to have the star-like brightness, must suddenly be transfigured as Christ was on Hermon.

The *Holy Grail* has been mentioned first because it is the most purely allegorical of the four in the volume. Attention is constantly kept upon the cup, and it connects and unifies the mystic meanings. *The Coming of Arthur,* however, as the opening poem, makes everything allegorical down to minute details.

4

The figure of the Lady of the Lake may be cited for the purpose of showing the freedom with which the scripture passages are handled.   The Lady is the Church, or the Spirit of God in the Church.   She knows a subtler magic than even Mage Merlin, the Intellect.   She handles Excalibur, the sword of the spirit, which is the Word of God.   She lives far down in the deep heart of things, but comes to the surface in troublous times and makes her presence felt.   The passages of Scripture which Tennyson uses in describing this Lady of the Lake are: *Revelation,* xiv, 2, " The voice of many waters "; *Isaiah,* xlviii, 18, "peace as a river, righteousness as... the sea "; *Matthew,* viii, 26, " He rebuked the . . . sea, and there was a great calm "; and *Matthew,* xiv, 25 " He went . . . walking upon the sea." Yet every one of these passages is present not only allusively, as in the second period, but in a form so altered that the very fact of allusion in any one case is almost open to argument.   The passage is as follows:

> And near him stood the Lady of the Lake,
> . . . .
> She gave the King his huge cross-hilted sword,
> Whereby to drive the heathen out. A mist
> Of incense curl'd about her, and her face
> Wellnigh was hidden in the minster gloom;
> But there was heard among the holy hymns
> A voice as of the waters, for she dwells
> Down in a deep—calm, whatsoever storms
> May shake the world—and when the surface rolls,
> Hath power to walk the waters like our Lord.
>
> (282-293)

So soon as the free and constructive hand of allegorizing is recognized the sources of the scriptural echoes become certain. The citations are unhesitatingly and even instinctively altered to suit the movements of the allegorical Lady of the Lake who dominates the picture, and the original imagery must be selected and altered so as to be kindred with the Lake of which she is the Lady.

3. The hazy and indefinite quality which the allegorical method communicates to the Scripture it uses may be illustrated

under a separate heading; for it casts light on the similar effect
of the allegorizing power upon other material in general. When
Arthur binds his knights with " simple words of great authority," the reader is at once reminded that Jesus " spake with
authority." [5] But the allusion is scarcely demonstrable. The
allegorizing creates an ambiguity. In *Pelleas and Ettarre*
Pelleas, suddenly wakened from his sleep in the woods,

> saw,
> Strange as to some old prophet might have seem'd
> A vision hovering on a sea of fire,
> Damsels in divers colors like the cloud
> Of sunset and sunrise.[6]

This is John on Patmos seeing his vision of those who stood on
the sea of glass mingled with fire. But the prophet is " some
old prophet" and the molten " glass " is not mentioned. The
allegorizing purpose generalizes everything and makes it indefinite. Under the inspiration of being knighted, Pelleas' coun-
tenance was so bright that men

> wonder'd after him, because his face
> Shone like the countenance of a priest of old
> Against the flame about a sacrifice
> Kindled by fire from heaven [7]

This points to the dedication of Solomon's temple. The anno-
tated editions of the idyll have notes to that effect. But after
all, the sacrifice *might* be Elijah's on Carmel. In fact the illuminated face *might* be that of some pagan priest. For they,
too, claimed to have descending fire. Always it is the irresistible
reminder with the doubt close at its heels. *The Passing of Arthur* contains two contrasted scripture citations which emphasize the contention here made. In the portion reprinted from
the 1842 edition is a simple and direct reference to the magi
with their gift of myrrh.[8] This way of using Scripture belongs

---

[5] *Coming of Arthur*, 260; *Matthew*, VII, 29.
[6] *Pelleas and Ettarre*, 48-52; *Revelation*, XV, 2.
[7] *Pelleas and Ettarre*, 136-139; 2 *Chronicles*, VII, 1.
[8] *Passing of Arthur*, 401 f.; *Matthew*, II, 11.

to the First Period and is an example of the simple method.
In the new portion of the idyll we have, by contrast, Arthur's
exclamation, " My God, thou hast forgotten me in my death." [9]
Surely this is an echo of Jesus' agonized cry upon the cross,
" My God, my God, why hast thou forsaken me ? " But is it,
really, after all ? There is no mention of the cross. There
is no definitely identifying detail of any kind. In this allegorizing period the Bible-passages call to us " like a friend's voice
from a distant field approaching in the darkness." [10] It is his
voice, but the sound is weird and unnatural. It is his voice,
but the expressions have lost their definiteness. Is it really he ?

4. The Allegorical Period is clearly marked off from the satirical one which followed it. Bitterness, satire, and pessimism
are more or less in evidence in these allegorical poems. But
they do not invade the uses of Scripture. It is with entire sincerity that Galahad cries when he determines to sit down in
Merlin's chair, " If I lose myself, I save myself." [11] Arthur
is not speaking ironically when he asks, " What go ye out into
the wilderness to see ? " [12] The biblical passages already cited
in this chapter may be searched in vain for any satirical element.
They are altered for purposes of description, of personification,
and of metaphysical theory, but not for purposes of satire.
Here, once more, the study of Tennyson's uses of Scripture
serves to show how clearly separated were the several stages of
his artistic development and method.

5. Tennyson's allegorical handling of Scripture is also instructive along technical lines. It shows how a literary artist
must handle his material in order to make a good allegory. The
method of the making might be equally clear in the case of
other allegories, if we had the original story or stories that
are used. Rückert's *Mann im Syrerland* is very impressive.
But the original story or stories of the camel, the spring, and the
mice are not at hand, or easily accessible. The artist's altera-

---

[9] *Passing of Arthur*, 27; *Matthew*, XXVII, 46.
[10] *Lancelot and Elaine*, 992 f.
[11] *Holy Grail*, 178; *Matthew*, X, 39.
[12] *Holy Grail*, 287; *Matthew*, XI, 7.

tions and blendings are not recognizable. But it is evident in the case of the personification of Humility, as cited above, how effective it is to tell her story in terms of the familiar stories of humble, biblical characters like the Wise Men of the East and of Jesus himself who was humble enough to leave the glories of heaven for the lowly places of the earth. It at once appears that an allegorical narrative gains effectiveness by utilizing material in already existing and *well known* stories that illustrate the principle, fact, or quality to be emphasized in the author's new creation. It also becomes evident how strong, free, and unfaltering must be the manipulating hand that moulds, creates, and unifies the narrative material.

6. The Allegorical Period then marks a distinct advance in Tennyson's artistic use of Scripture. The first period shows one passage at a time imaginatively re-created with faithfulness to the original statements. The second period combines condensed allusions to various passages into single, poetic conceptions of which the unity is in some non-scriptural idea or purpose. The component passages and images are, however, still used in their primary or scriptural sense. Each combination, like a mosaic, makes a pattern or picture of its own; but the pieces of material are used in their natural color as they come to the artist's hand and are, therefore, clearly recognizable and easy of identification. In the third period, however, the scripture material is freely altered, blended with other material from Scripture, and with material from outside sources. A dominating artistic purpose, moreover, uses all the material as color for its brush. It is the difference between a mosaic, which does not change the colors it uses, and a painting, in which colors taken from a palette are freely blended, mixed, and shaded into a picture with an action and meaning of its own. Painting is, after all, a higher and more creative art than the making of mosaics. The intellectual power and artistic strength of Tennyson are greater in the Allegorical Period than in the earlier ones.

CHAPTER IV

The Period of Satire and Pessimism

Tennyson like Shakespeare had his satirical and pessimistic period. The evidences of disillusion and discouragement of spirit are scarcely plainer in *Macbeth, Lear,* and *Antony and Cleopatra* than they are in the productions of Tennyson's corresponding years. Almost every poem shows strong evidence of sadness, bitterness, and pessimism. The satirical mood was not, indeed, wholly absent from any of the three preceding periods. But, after all, examples drawn from those periods do not serve to destroy the distinctness of this succeeding one. On the contrary, they help to define its special quality and to make its general chronological limits more distinct.

I. (a) By the satirical use of Scripture is not here meant any mere tavern-made allusion, however irreverent, to being " saved by works," [1] or to a skeleton as " God's image, the ground plan," [2] or the convivial light-mindedness of the drinker at an inn who imagines himself to be in Paul's third heaven.[3] These are mere artistic by-plays, youthful touches, which indicate no fixed mood. The satire, such as it is, is good-humored.

(b) Nor are hypocritical uses of biblical language included here, for hypocrisy by such uses pays the good book a genuine tribute.

When Vivien says she is " seethed like a kid in its mother's milk,"[4] she means Merlin to take her at her word and to be affected by the biblical warning against treating people as she is being treated. The swindler in *Sea Dreams* misses his mark,

---

[1] *The Vision of Sin,* 91; *Galatians,* II, 16.
[2] *The Vision of Sin,* 187; *Genesis,* I, 26.
[3] *Will Waterproof,* 70; *2 Corinthians,* XII, 2.
[4] *Merlin and Vivien,* 867; *Exodus,* XXIII, 19.

to be sure, but his aim is serious when in good Bible-phrases he begs the city clerk to have faith in the honesty of his mining-schemes and connects the books he keeps with the great books of the judgment-day.[5]

(c) Nor, again, is even honest-hearted satire here intended. The molten torrent of Averill's scripture satire and sarcasm in *Aylmer's Field* is an honest torrent. The satire is pointed toward his audience. It is free from even the slightest satirical disposition toward the sacred text. The sense of satire arises directly from making confessedly horrible practices recorded in the Bible parallel to sins which modern society countenances and upholds. The whole sermon rather than any specific lines is evidence of the fact.

(d) Nor, fourthly, is here meant by the satirical use of Scripture any merely general satirical or pessimistic effect secured by allusion to biblical passages. The bad voice, for example, drew a satirical picture of the man who called himself a little lower than the angels,[6] and of his children coming to honor or to shame after his death [7] while he himself was forgotten by the very places that had known him.[8] But these effects do not imply any misinterpretation of the Bible even by bad persons. In all these earlier uses, however effective, Scripture is taken by the character that uses it in its fair, scriptural sense. A sad, cold, or bitter biblical allusion represents a sad, cold, or bitter fact, real or alleged. The use, even the trivial or despairing or sarcastic use, is mentally honest. In *The Palace of Art,* for example, the masses are, indeed, compared to the swine of Gadara,[9] but the common people, as the egoistic soul sees them, are a fair counterpart to the wallowing and brainless creatures.

2. What *is* meant in this study by the satirical use of Scripture, as distinguished from the earlier uses just outlined, is

---

[5] *Sea Dreams,* 148-155; *Daniel,* VII, 10; *Galatians,* II, 20; *Romans,* I, 17; *Romans,* VIII, 28 (see p. 40 for the passage).

[6] *Two Voices,* 198 f.; *Psalms,* VIII, 5.

[7] *Two Voices,* 256; *Job,* XIV, 21.

[8] *Two Voices,* 264; *Psalms,* CIII, 16.

[9] *Palace of Art,* 201 f.; *Luke,* VIII, 33.

the set and fixed perversion of it in the mouth and in the meaning of the character who cites it.   Bitter is deliberately put for
sweet and sweet for bitter.   The attitude toward Scripture is
fierce and depraved or at best utterly pessimistic and hopeless.
There is a slight prophecy of this rough usage in Gawain's oath,
" Christ kill me, then, but I will slice him handless by the
wrist ";[10] but within the period itself the satirical roughness is
much more definite and intensified.   In *The Last Tournament*
the Red Knight howled and

> Sware by the scorpion-worm that twists in hell
> And stings itself to everlasting death.[11]

In the same idyll Dagonet voices the pessimism of the story by
saying that some of Arthur's knights had grown

> So witty that they play'd at ducks and drakes
> With Arthur's vows on the great lake of fire.[12]

Of Arthur himself, he says:

> Ay, ay, my brother fool, the king of fools!
> Conceits himself as God that he can make
> Figs out of thistles.[13]

In a most ugly way, also, Tristram applies to Dagonet the one
passage of which the seemingly scornful and low allusion makes
it a solitary exception on the lips of Jesus, " For I have flung
thee pearls and find thee swine." [14]   *Balin and Balan,* published
in 1885, strikes the same note in reference to scriptural matters.
The sun-worship will beat the cross to earth.[15]   When Vivien
ceased talking to Balin, his evil spirit leapt upon him.[16]   Vivien
herself better prizes the living dog than the dead lion.[17]   Now it
is not merely the position of the idylls just quoted in the series

---

[10] *Pelleas and Ettarre*, 329 f. (1869).
[11] *The Last Tournament*, 450 f.; *Isaiah*, LXVI, 24.
[12] *The Last Tournament*, 344 f.; *Revelation*, XX, 10, 14 f.
[13] *The Last Tournament*, 354 f.; *Matthew*, VII, 16.
[14] *The Last Tournament*, 310; *Matthew*, VII, 6.
[15] *Balin and Balan*, 452; *Philippians*, III, 18.
[16] *Balin and Balan*, 529; *Acts*, XIX, 16.
[17] *Balin and Balan*, 573 f.; *Ecclesiastes*, IX, 4.

as an organic whole or as a complex allegory that limits their uses of Scripture to these bitter strains; for *Guinevere* belongs in the same general place as *The Last Tournament,* and the biblical references in *Guinevere,* however sad they must necessarily be, are none of them satirical, but they are simple, tender, and even touched with hope.

3. Nearly if not quite all the fine strong poems of these later years are sad and bitter. They are pierced thru and thru by the tragedy of life. The fact is sharply emphasized by the way Scripture is utilized in all those that make any clear or outstanding use of it at all. The agony of suffering motherhood moans thru *Rizpah.* What misery, what madness, what accumulated fierceness of her single instinctive passion Willy's dying mother expresses! How she sweeps every passage of the Bible that she recalls, or her well-meaning visitor reads, into the torrent of her own bitter story! "As the tree falls, so must it lie." [18] But one by one she has gathered all the bones of her boy as they fell from the gallows' chain. What else was there left to "fall"? "Bone of my bones and flesh of my flesh," said Adam of Eve, but all the mother could make the passage mean was that the ravens and other birds had picked away the flesh of her boy from the gallows and left only the bones: "Flesh of my flesh was gone, but bone of my bone was left."[19] "Full of compassion and mercy—long-suffering," [20] read the visitor from the Psalm. But the mother can connect long-suffering only with the long-time hanging of Willy's body in the mist and the wind and the shower and the snow. Then she goes past the biblical phrases into theological doctrines, election and reprobation, and then past the doctrines to God Himself and so gets back into the heart of the Bible again. But it is all done in spite of the Bible, as it were, and by changing the Bible's meanings. It is not the biblical expressions that give her any hope but rather her own instincts taking her back

---

[18] *Rizpah,* 12; *Ecclesiastes,* XI, 3.
[19] *Rizpah,* 51; *Genesis,* II, 23.
[20] *Rizpah,* 63; *Psalms,* LXXXVI, 15; CXI, 4; CXII, 4; CXLV, 8.

of the expressions and even into opposition to them. *Rizpah* is a poem of motherhood in an agony and desolation which polarize, and we may fairly say pervert, with artistic power every sacred verse they recall or hear.

In *The Children's Hospital* the coarse red surgeon says, " The good Lord Jesus has had his day." He who said, " Little children should come to me," [21] saves Emmie before the surgeon comes,—saves her by her death.

Sir John Oldcastle, a Wiclifite refugee in the Welsh mountains, recites his situation in many a biblical quotation and allusion. One of them pleasantly enough compares Lutterworth to Bethlehem. In it the word was born again.[22] The Bible, fulfilling Pentecost,[23] uses the tongues of all the world; but it will bring to men not peace, but a sword, a fire.[24] Antichrist is in power.[25] Sir John knows that he is to pass in the fire of Babylon.[26] The form of a fourth like the Son of God was with the Hebrew three in the furnace. They were not burnt.

> Those three! the fourth
> Was like the Son of God! Not burnt were they.
> On *them* the smell of burning had not past.[27]

But Oldcastle cites the passage in order to say that he himself will not be saved in that way.

In *Columbus* the poet does not paint the great voyages and marvelous discoveries of the explorer, but sees his hero in chains, or bed-ridden, insulted and persecuted, a source of danger even to a visitor. The scriptural passages emphasize the Bible's scientific errors. The Psalmist's conception of the earth's shape was wrong.[28] " Two Adams was clean against

---

[21] *In the Children's Hospital,* vi; *Matthew,* xix, 14.
[22] *Sir John Oldcastle,* 24-27; *Micah,* v, 2; *John,* i, 14.
[23] *Sir John Oldcastle,* 33; *Acts,* ii, 1-4.
[24] *Sir John Oldcastle,* 36; *Matthew,* x, 34.
[25] *Sir John Oldcastle,* 72; *1 John,* ii, 18.
[26] *Sir John Oldcastle,* 118; *Daniel,* iii, 6.
[27] *Sir John Oldcastle,* 167-169; *Daniel,* iii, 25.
[28] *Columbus,* 46 f; *Psalms,* civ, 2.

God's word." [29] Columbus must suffer as God's son had suffered.[30]

The Wreck quotes " Thou hast sinned,[31] and the despairing woman says " the wages of sin is death "[32] and " I am the Jonah. The crew should cast me into the deep." [33]

In *Despair* the suicidal skeptics think Christ preaches hell rather than good news,[34] God is a fireless pillar of smoke,[35] man is a worm writhing in the dust,[36] prayer is taking the name of God in vain,[37] the sun and moon of science are both turned to blood,[38] and man is foreknown and foredoomed to everlasting hell by God's arbitrary will.[39]

The fire and beauty of these *" Ballads and Other Poems "* are evidence of Tennyson's still radiant genius, but it is a sad and bitter radiance. Nothing is normal or gladsome. Nothing has a happy issue. This fact is evident from a general reading of the poems, but it is brought into still more striking relief by the dark and sinister type of most of the scriptural passages used, and by the general perversion of the few passages of a brighter tone.

4. There are two antithetical facts that give striking evidence of the satirical quality of the fourth period in Tennyson's artistic use of Scripture. The first fact is the absence of biblical allusions from *Gareth and Lynnette,* published in 1872. This idyll contains no Scripture except in small phrasings. Its position as the first idyll in the series requires gaiety, boldness, and vivacity. It is, of course, in view of its date, highly allegorical. In fact it is the only one of the idylls where any of the characters have, as in *Bunyan,* descriptive names, such as Night,

---

[29] *Columbus,* 53 f.; *Genesis,* I, 27 (cf. *1 Corinthians,* xv, 45).
[30] *Columbus,* 150-152; *Matthew,* x, 23-25.
[31] *The Wreck,* 88; *Habakkuk,* II, 10.
[32] *The Wreck,* 93; *Romans,* VI, 23.
[33] *The Wreck,* 94; *Jonah,* I, 15.
[34] *Despair,* 25 f.; *Matthew,* xxv, 46.
[35] *Despair,* 29; *Exodus,* XIII, 21.   [37] *Despair,* 52; *Exodus,* xx, 7.
[36] *Despair,* 30-32; *Job,* xxv, 6.   [38] *Despair,* 91; *Joel,* II, 31.
[39] *Despair,* 96 f.; *Matthew,* xx, 15; *Romans,* VIII, 29.

Day, and Death. But *The Holy Grail* which is also highly
allegorical, makes much and important use of Scripture. Does
not the contrast, in this respect, between the two idylls find its
cause in the difference of the periods in which they were written?
However bright and happy in intention *Gareth and Lynette*
may be, it was written when the only strong and vigorous artistic use of Scripture of which the poet seemed capable was the
satirical or pessimistic one. In so glad a story, however, only
some cheerful biblical incident or hopeful landscape could ap-
propriately be used. Satirical and pessimistic allusions to the
Bible would have been out of place. Hence there are no very
definite allusions to it at all.

The second and contrasted fact is the use of Scripture in
Merlin and Vivien. The poet printed six trial copies of this
idyll in 1857 and it was published in 1859. It therefore distinctly belongs to the Period of Simplicity. Yet at the very
beginning of the idyll in its present form we find no less than
three examples of the bitterest satire at the expense of the Bible.
A wandering minstrel at Tintagil reports that there are ascetic
knights in Arthur's court who have taken

> vows like theirs that high in heaven
> Love most, but neither marry nor are given
> In marriage, angels of our Lord's report.[40]

The words of Jesus, here referred to, constitute his clearest
and most spiritual description of the heavenly life of the resur-
rection-state. The poet, however, makes the minstrel's citation
merely a satirical foil for Mark's ugly comment, " Here are
snakes within the grass." A few lines further Vivien repu-
diates the idea that she is afraid to go to Arthur's court:

> Fear them? no,
> As love, if love be perfect, casts out fear,
> So hate, if hate be perfect, casts out fear.[41]

The words here alluded to contain one of the Bible's strongest
as well as briefest descriptions of the perfect peace that belongs

---

[40] *Merlin and Vivien*, 14-16; *Matthew*, XXII, 30.
[41] *Merlin and Vivien*, 39-41; *1 John*, IV, 18.

to perfect devotion. But, as Vivien uses the verse, it gives her
hatred of goodness a striking intensity. Once more, and only
a few lines further on, she assails Arthur himself. She does
it on the authority of the Bible:

> There is no being pure,
> My cherub; saith not Holy Writ the same? [42]

But her citation is, of course, absolutely satirical. Here, then,
three of the loftiest statements of Scripture in regard to the
heavenly life, the peace that passeth understanding, and the
prevalence of sin, are used to point the most gross and bitter
satire. The perversion of the best is worst. The degradation
of the highest goes lowest. These satirical uses of Scripture
in the mouths of Mark and Vivien paint them as the extremes
of foulness and bitterness. To harmonize such uses of Scripture
with the simple and beautiful references in the same idyll
to woman's curiosity [43] and to the sin and psalms of David [44]
constitutes in itself something of an artistic difficulty, but the
question in point here is, how could such intense and complex
satire in the use of Scripture appear in an idyll of the earliest
group? The answer from the point of view of this study is
as striking as it is obvious. These references did *not* appear
in the idyll as first printed. They appeared for the first time
in the edition of 1874. In other words they are the direct product of Tennyson's fourth, or satiric and pessimistic, period. It
is not easy to conceive of a more illuminating proof of the satirical and pessimistic attitude toward all things, which controlled
Tennyson during this period, than these two antithetical facts
stated above: first, he could not or did not put into the bright
new idyll, which he wrote at this time and assigned to the first
position in the series, a single clear and outstanding reference
of any kind to Holy Writ, because only bright and cheery
references were admissible, and he now seems to have become
incapable of such; and secondly, he could go back seventeen

---

[42] *Merlin and Vivien*, 51, 52; *Romans*, III, 10 et al.
[43] *Merlin and Vivien*, 360 f.; *Genesis*, III, 12.
[44] *Merlin and Vivien*, 760-4; *2 Samuel* XI.

years to an idyll of which the position and character did admit
of satire and insert in it as an introduction three of the Bible's
loftiest sayings and use them in such a way as to convert them
into the most conscienceless, depraved, and repulsive satire.

5. The immediately preceding remarks have been made concerning Tennyson as an artist rather than as a man. But in
his case artist and man are so blended that it may be well to
add what seems to be the explanation of the facts encountered
in this, his satirical period. Tennyson's art was marked by
simplicity and sincerity. He took up no subject in which he
was not veritably involved. His poetry was "the legitimate
child of natural thought and natural feeling. Vital sincerity
or living correspondence between idea and form" was his to
an unusual degree. He was also in deep sympathy with the
varying moods of his century. His mind entered insertively
into its successive changes and varieties of faith and doubt as
if they were his own. Milton's writings were deeply affected
by his personal experiences and by the stirring events of his
lifetime. His own blindness, the disorders of the London streets,
and the struggle for liberty are clearly reflected in his poetry
and his prose. It is no less true that Tennyson's literary work
was profoundly affected by the theological movements, the scientific discoveries, and the agnostic philosophies, which spread
like great waves thru England during his poetical career. The
skepticism of the time touched him. He felt the strain of
doubt. He clung to faith, yet sometimes felt himself almost
wrenched away from it. More than one critic has interpreted
the wife's vision of the tide in *Sea-Dreams* as a picture of the
inroads of skepticism. From earliest years he was capable of
strong disbelief and intense pessimism. A set and fixed mater-
ialism makes up the preponderating bulk of *The Two Voices*.
The very force of his fight against it shows the power he felt
in its assaults. The poem was written in 1833 in "a period
of great depression consequent upon the death of his sister."
It does, indeed, embody a mood which he underwent and over-
came. But the enemy was clothed in hardened skins and would

not receive a mortal wound. Even *In Memoriam's* doubtful triumph emerges from fierce struggles. Many a skeptical passage in it is prophetic of recurrence. Such recurrence or recrudescence is clear in the later idylls. These facts seem to explain this fourth method or stage which appears in Tennyson's use of the Bible. The general scientific skepticism which flourished in the times of his mid-career was closely concerned with Scripture. It seemed to discredit *Genesis,* the poetic home of *Paradise Lost* and, to no small extent, of Tennyson himself. It said that " miracles do not happen." It regarded the forms of faith and worship as useful, after a fashion, for inferior minds, but not to be taken seriously by men of mental strength and courage. For God could not really be known in any such definite way as the Bible and the church declared. When a poet, for whatever reason, becomes a genuine representative of his age, he gives great hostages. He may be required to feel its doubts, its fears, and its transitions. A time came—perhaps it came earlier than is commonly supposed—when Tennyson could no longer enter with unclouded joy into the ideal scenes of the Bible. The mist that went up from the heart of that Eden no longer kept it green but clung to it like a face-cloth to the face and classed it with the dead. It was no longer possible for so sincere a man to enter with warm sympathetic gladness into the biblical scenes and incidents. But for an artist whose poetry was so natural and legitimate a product of his heart some such entrance was necessary for beautiful portrayals. Hence they ceased. One form of honest use of biblical matter was, however, still left. It was the satirical and pessimistic use. For the Bible stands for ideal goodness and hope. Its phrases can still be put with entire artistic fitness and with intellectual honesty into the mouths of the pessimistic and the corrupt. It is only required that the characters that use the scripture passages should use them with complete disbelief or scorn. The sense must be ironical, sarcastic, despairing. When one knows by experience, as Tennyson surely did, the mood of skepticism and despair, he can project himself into it and portray it with artistic vividness and strength. It is this use of Scripture in which Tennyson now becomes powerful as never before. He seems never to have had that robust and enduring faith which enabled Browning to throw himself into the heart of a biblical character or situation. He could not write a *Saul* or a *Death in the Desert*. Browning handled Scripture in substantially the same fashion thruout his life, largely because his attitude toward it never seriously changed. The fluctuations of Tennyson's faith, on the other hand, seem to have played a large part in dividing his artistic use of Scripture into the stages or phases discriminated in this study. It is not, of course, to be assumed that Tennyson or any other poet necessarily feels toward the Bible or any other great subject in the way he pictures the characters of his poems as feeling. But the direction in which his mind is moving may be to no small extent the explanation of his artistic method at any particular time. Tennyson could enter into the cynical, satirical, and pessimistic use of Scripture at this time because of the struggles in his own mind and perhaps because of his personal trials and losses. In any case, the artistic mood and method are clearly defined, and observation of them within the province of his uses of Scripture helps us to understand the general sadness and bitterness of human life, with which he so deeply sympathized during these years.

CHAPTER V.

The Dramatic Period.

Chronological facts require the recognition of a dramatic period in Tennyson's artistic career. For the dates of the dramas are not distributed here and there among those of his other works. The three long plays that make the " historic trilogy " appeared in 1875, 1877, and 1879 when the poet was sixty-six, sixty-eight, and seventy years of age respectively. Even the shorter dramas followed rather quickly. *The Falcon* was played at the St. James Theater in 1879. *The Cup* was begun in 1879, and *The Promise of May* was produced at the Globe Theatre in 1882. *The Foresters,* however, for which Tennyson himself said he did not care as he did for *Becket* and *Harold,*[1] was not published till much later. With this unimportant exception the dramas are confined to a relatively short period and represent a concentrated movement of the poet's genius in his later years.

The accumulated intensity and power with which Tennyson flung himself into these dramatic productions is indicated in several ways. He undertook them against the advice of his best friends. He persisted in writing them in the face of their failure upon the stage. He was undaunted by the hostility of the stage critics and even of the people at large.[2] He was determined to be a working playwright and desired the most prominent actors and actresses to put his dramas before the public. And, finally, his extreme depression at the ill-success of his plays in the theaters was beyond all reason for one whose general fame was so secure. The present study furnishes an incidental confirmation and illustration of the gathered strength and resources which the poet put into his dramas. For they afford examples of all except one of the successive stages in Tenny-

---

[1] *Memoir,* II, 390.

[2] See *e. g.*, Edmund Gosse in the *Encyc. Brit.*, Eleventh Ed., Art. *Tennyson.*

son's use of Scripture. The single exception is the use that characterised the Period of Simplicity. By a kind of psychological necessity that one method is lacking in the dramas. But there are abounding examples of Combination, Allegory, and Satire. The dramas, in fact, furnish a species of summary, or recapitulation, of the artistic uses of Scripture already distinguished and illustrated. This is one defence of the separate consideration of them in this study. The term " dramatic " is not, of course, homogeneous with " simple," " combined," " allegorical," and " satirical." A method of using literary material is not a species of literature. The various and contrasted characters of a drama, or of a collection of dramas, might use Scripture in any of the ways above mentioned. This supposition is close to the actual fact in the case of Tennyson. If the dramas had been distributed thruout the poet's career, a drama from the period of simplicity would doubtless have contained illustrations of the simple use, and a drama from the period of combination examples of that form of use. A corresponding fact would also have obtained in dramas from each of the two later periods. But the dramas being a gathered and concentrated output of the poet's genius in all other available respects are such in the matter of Scripture also and hence furnish examples of all three later uses.

1. Tennyson's perfected artistic power with scripture language now enables him to make effective combinations in both monolog and dialog. A striking example of the former is found in the dying words of Edward the Confessor:

> It is finished
> I have built the Lord a house—the Lord hath dwelt
> In darkness. I have built the Lord a house—
> Palms, flowers, pomegranates, golden cherubim
> With twenty-cubit wings from wall to wall—
> I have built the Lord a house—sing, Asaph! clash
> The cymbal, Heman! blow the trumpet, priest!
> Fall, cloud, and fill the house—lo! my two pillars,
> Jachin and Boaz! [3]

---

[3] *Harold*, III, i, 101-109; *John*, XIX, 30; *1 Kings*, VIII, 12; VI, 27-29; VII, 42; VIII, 20; *1 Chron.*, XXV, 1; *2 Chron.*, VII, 1; *1 Kings*, VIII, 10; *1 Kings*, VII, 21.

Mary, in like manner, can combine Scripture in exultation over her child.[4] Pole can do it in his official, ecclesiastical way,[5] Gardinar in his brutal way,[6] Cole in his cruelly hypocritical way,[7] and Cranmer with true piety in his last defence.[8]

The combinations effected thru dialog range all the way from the whimsical interchanges between Fitzurse and the Third Beggar to the high talk of Herbert and Becket concerning the devil's " if " and Becket's treading the wine-press alone. The two contrasted passages may be quoted as illustrations:

Fitzurse. Sheep, said he? And sheep without the shepherd, too. Where is my lord archbishop? Thou the lustiest and lousiest of this Cain's brotherhood, answer.

Third Beggar. With Cain's answer, my lord. Am I his keeper? Thou shouldst call him Cain, not me.

Fitzurse. So I do, for he would murder his brother the State.

Third Beggar (rising and advancing). No, my lord; but because the Lord hath set his mark upon him that no man should murder him.

Fitzurse. Where is he? where is he?

Third Beggar. With Cain belike, in the land of Nod, or in the land of France for aught I know.[9]

* * * * * *

Walter Map. And is the king's *if* too high a stile for your lordship to overstep and come at all things in the next field?

Becket. Ay, if this *if* be like the devil's ' *if*
Thou wilt fall down and worship me.'

Herbert.   O, Thomas,
I could fall down and worship thee, my Thomas,
For thou hast trodden this wine-press alone.

Becket. Nay, of the people there are many with me.[10]

---

[4] *Queen Mary*, III, ii, 97-100; *Isaiah*, IX, 6; I, 24; *Numbers*, XXIV, 17. *Queen Mary*, 109-113; *Numbers*, XXIV, 17; *Psalms*, XXIV, 7.

[5] *Queen Mary*, III, iii, 114-136; *Luke*, XV, 10; *John*, III, 17; *Matthew*, V, 17; *Micah*, VII, 19; *Matthew*, XIII, 8; *Revelation*, V, 9; I, 5; XIX, 7; *Ephesians*, V, 23.

[6] *Queen Mary*, III, iv, 18-20; *Luke*, XIV, 23; *Galatians*, V, 12; *2 Corinthians*, III, 6.

[7] *Queen Mary*, IV, iii, 55-61; *Galatians*, I, 24; *Luke*, XXIII, 43; *Daniel*, IV, 20-28; *Luke*, VI, 14.

[8] *Queen Mary*, IV, iii, 119-129; *1 Peter*, II, 13 f.; *Romans*, XIII, 4; *Galatians*, VI, 10; *1 John*, IV, 16, 20.

[9] *Becket*, I, iv, 170-186; *Matthew*, IX, 36; *Genesis*, IV, 9-15; *Genesis*, IV, 16.

[10] *Becket*, III, iii, 210-217; *Matthew*, IV, 9; *Isaiah*, LXIII, 3.

2. Scriptural allegorizing also appears in these dramas. Becket reproaches Henry:

> The spouse of the Great King, thy King, hath fallen—
> The daughter of Zion lies beside the way—
> The priests of Baäl tread her underfoot—[11]

Mary's willingness to restore the Roman Church to England is described in terms which allegorize the incident of Peter's continued knocking at the gate of the apostolic Mary's house.[12] In all such passages the dramas revive the free alteration, the uncertain certainty, the indefinite definiteness, and the elusive allusiveness which characterized the use of biblical texts in the allegorizing parts of the Idylls.

3. The satirical and pessimistic notes are the strongest. Almost every extended allusion is dark or fierce or hypocritical or homicidal. Even the allegorizing is sad or despairing and frequently belongs under the head of satire also, or of pessimism. The *Memoir* speaks of the difficulty of giving sufficient " relief " to the intense sadness of *Queen Mary*. " Nothing less than the holy calm of the meek and penitent Cranmer can be adequate artistic relief." [13]   But Cranmer's references to Scripture are not only hortatory and heroic but joyless and sad. A much more adequate " artistic relief " might perhaps have been found in some happy scripture portrayal islanded in the midst of these bitter waters. Tennyson knew how to find artistic relief for the sadness of *In Memoriam* in the bright picture of the supper in Lazarus' honor. There are many other biblical pictures which, if wrought with equal genius, after the manner of the period of simplicity, would have afforded the needed feeling of happy contrast. Elizabeth could have given one out of her earlier days. The milkmaid, too, was available. In *Becket* Margery was familiar enough with the garden of Eden [14] and knew how to make a happy song from non-scriptural material.[15]

---

[11] *Becket*, III, iii, 151-153; *Revelation*, XXI, 9; *Isaiah*, I, 8; *Isaiah*, LI, 20, 23; *2 Kings*, X, 19.

[12] *Queen Mary*, III, ii, 38-44; *Acts*, XII, 12-17.

[13] *Memoir*, II, 179.   [14] *Becket*, III, i, 90-94.   [15] *Becket*, III, i, 50-61.

It surely is instructive as to Tennyson's attitude toward Scripture in these days that he did not insert in these dramas any bright song or scene or story from the Bible.

Some of the satirical and bitter uses are exceedingly powerful and seem to recall the late insertions at the beginning of *Merlin and Vivien.* In *Queen Mary,* Paget and Howard are talking of the rocking and reeling action and reaction of the times. Paget uses *Isaiah.*

> My Lord, the world is like a drunken man,
> Who cannot move straight to his end, but reels
> Now to the right, then as far to the left,
> Push'd by the crowd beside—and underfoot
> An earthquake; for since Henry for a doubt—
> Which a young lust had clapt upon the back,
> Crying, ' Forward '—set our old church rocking, men
> Have hardly known what to believe, or whether
> They should believe in anything.[16]

Drunk in an earthquake! Could satirical despair find a more perfect figure for the situation!—When Jesus rose from the dead he appeared first to Mary Magdalene. He had entered the divine life of the resurrection but had not yet ascended to the right hand of God. In the mouths of the assassins as they seize Becket the extreme sublimity of the scene is turned to the extreme of satire.

> *Becket.* Touch me not!
> *De Brito.* How the good priest gods himself!
>   He is not yet ascended to the Father.[17]

Could there be a fiercer or more murderous satire in scripture terms than this perversion of spiritual affection into deadly hate! The scripture passages cited thus far in this chapter are only a few among many uncited ones. But they are sufficient to show that while the poet summoned up all his artistic powers with Scripture (as with all other literary material) in order to make these dramas great, the satirical feeling that lay in his

---

[16] *Queen Mary,* IV, iii, 252-260. Cf. *Isaiah,* XXIV, 20, and XXVIII, 7, for the imagery.

[17] *Becket,* v, iii, 76-78; *John,* XX, 17.

mind betrays itself, nevertheless, in all three forms of use. The dramas, as remarked above, furnish a summary of them, but it is, after all, a satirical summary.

It should perhaps be added that the dramas very naturally afford something like a summary or revival of the *characters* who use Scripture in the earlier periods. Cranmer's religious use of the Bible, for example, recalls Enoch Arden's,[18] and Cole's hypocritical use recalls the impostor in *Sea Dreams*.[19] But the portrayals in the dramas are so much fuller and stronger that they suggest a large advance in intellectual range and in power of wielding literary knowledge.

There is a second and more compelling reason for studying the dramas by themselves. It is their relation to Shakespeare's. Three facts seem to compel a comparison of the two. First, Shakespeare was confessedly Tennyson's inspiration. Secondly, it was the laureate's avowed purpose to complete the line of Shakespeare's Chronicle plays. Thirdly, certain scenes and situations in Tennyson's dramas are parallel to certain ones in Shakespeare and thus invite comparison of artistic methods.

1. Tennyson from his earliest period regarded Shakespeare as the one great soul among the immortal dead. Hallam, in heaven, was conversing with the great souls of all time. But there was one supreme name among them, tho even to him Tennyson would not yield in love.

> I loved thee, Spirit, and love, nor can
> The soul of Shakespeare love thee more.[20]

Beside this intensely concrete and mystic reference may be put the last scenes recorded in the *Memoir* " On Wednesday the 29th [of September] . . . I drove with him to Haslemere. He would point out his old accustomed haunts saying ' I shall never walk these again.' . . . He read *Job* and *St. Matthew*. . . . On Monday morning at 8 o'clock he sent me for his *Shakespeare*. I took him Steevens' Edition, *Lear, Cymbeline,*

---

[18] Compare *Queen Mary*, IV, iii, 77-151 with *Enoch Arden*, 220-226.
[19] Compare *Queen Mary*, IV, iii, 39-69 with *Sea Dreams*, 148-155.
[20] *In Memoriam*, LXI.

and *Troilus and Cressida,* three plays which he loved dearly. He read two or three lines and told Dr. Dabbs he never should get well again. . . . Later, at his request, I read some *Shakespeare* to him. . . . Dr. Dabbs who had been in London for the day had seen Irving. On his return my father remarked ' What is he doing with my *Becket?* It will be successful on the stage with Irving as Becket.' . . . Tuesday . . . at noon he called out ' Where is my *Shakespeare?* I must have my *Shakespeare.'* . . . On Wednesday . . . he begged for his *Shakespeare* again. . . . At two o'clock he again asked for his *Shakespeare* and lay with his hand resting on it open and tried to read it. . . . His last food was taken at a quarter to four and he tried to read but could not. He exclaimed ' I have opened it.' Whether this referred to the *Shakespeare* opened by him . . . I cannot tell. . . . Thursday Oct. 6th at 1.35 A. M. the great poet breathed his last . . . his hand clasping the *Shakespeare* which he had asked for but recently and which he had kept by him to the end. . . . We placed *Cymbeline* with him and a laurel wreath from Virgil's tomb."[21]

These broken quotations, including the mention of *Becket,* show how intensely Tennyson loved *Shakespeare* and how closely he associated him with his own dramatic work. The explanation of his determined toil upon his three historic dramas may lie in the fact that the soul of Shakespeare had been working in his soul for many years. Critics of Tennyson observe how adroitly he could bend the study of *Shakespeare* to the enrichment of his personal style.[22] Even as a boy of fourteen he had written plays. May it not be that all through his career he had looked forward to the dramatic field as the culminating place of his work and that it was the inspiration of *Shakespeare* that at last took its delayed effect in his dramas ?

2. Tennyson must have realized that his attempt to complete the line of Shakespeare's Chronicle-plays which end with the commencement of the Reformation, would inevitably invite com-

---

[21] *Memoir,* II, 425-429.
[22] Edmund Gosse in Encyc. Brit., Art. *Tennyson.*

parison between the two authors. It is no wrong to him therefore, if this study compares the two dramatists within the province of their respective methods with Scripture. It is, as it
were, an acceptance of an invitation.

3. The recurrence of certain features in Shakespeare's plays
in those of Tennyson suggests a comparison as well as an inspiration. *Harold* opens with the description of a comet and its
varying effects upon the superstitious and the sensible. The
opening lines of *The First Part of Henry VI* make use of the
same astronomical phenomenon. Comets are indeed common
property for poets. Milton refers to their " horrid hair " and
Shakespeare to their " crystal tresses." But it is scarcely as
common to open a drama with the appearance of a comet as a
menace to a kingdom. Again, the sequence of ghosts, Edward,
Wulfnoth, Tostig, and the Norman saints, which appear to
Harold on the eve of battle, strongly reminds the reader of the
ghosts of Henry, Clarence, the trio (Rivers, Grey, and Vaughan), Hastings, Annie, and Buckingham appearing to Richard
and Richmond.[23] Harold's sane remark that the comet is seen
by all the world as well as England and threatens the English
no more than it does the French and Normans recalls Richard's
insistence that the self-same sun that frowns on him looks sadly
upon Richmond![24] In *Queen Mary* Cleopatra's barge seems
to float not far away from that of Pole.[25] Many other parallels
might be cited. But these three are sufficient to indicate
roughly what is meant by the soul of Shakespeare working in
the soul of Tennyson. A somewhat closer notice of each of
them, moreover, points us toward the general difference that
will appear between Tennyson's and Shakespeare's uses of
Scripture. Tennyson's comet, like those in *Shakespeare,* por-
tends great political events. But Shakespeare's reference
exhibits a single sharp action:

---

[23] *Queen Mary,* III, ii, 4-20; *Antony and Cleopatra,* II, ii, 196-218.

[24] *Harold,* I, i, 67-71; *Richard Third,* v, iii, 283-288.

[25] *Queen Mary,* III, ii, 4-20; *Antony and Cleopatra,* II, ii, 196-218.

They brandish their crystal tresses in the sky
And with them scourge the bad revolting stars
That have consented unto Henry's death.[26]

In *Harold* the comet is a "treble-brandished scourge." There
is a star that dances in it as if mad with agony. The flame
either streams upward from the abyss or floats downward from
the throne of God. Here are three separate conceptions in
place of Shakespeare's single one. Tennyson's picture is fuller
and richer in detail but lacks the direct force of a single stroke
which Shakespeare's has. Tennyson's comet moreover recurs at
various other places in the play.[27] Shakespeare's has flashed before us once for all. In something the same way Shakespeare uses
Scripture with single, sharp, and isolated strokes while Tennyson distributes it over a wider area in a drama. The ghosts
that appear to Richard and Richmond before the battle strike
each one blow with the same hammer of retribution for Richard's blood-guiltiness and hold out the same hope of victory to
Richmond. But in Harold's night-vision Edward is a messen-
ger of love, Wulfnoth of vain regret, Tostig of revenge, and the
Norman saints of superstition. The blows are lighter than
those of Shakespeare's ghosts, come from different directions,
and fall on different spots. There is a kind of parallel to this
in the way scripture passages of the same type or working
toward the same end are concentrated upon a single character
in certain of Shakespeare's plays, while in *Tennyson* the passages exhibit greater variety and are connected with more than
one character in the same play. The two barges referred to
above are another illustration of the same general fact. In
both cases there is a great wealth of imagery and of descriptive
detail. But in Shakespeare's lines nothing tends to distract
attention from the one figure of Cleopatra seated on the barge.
Everybody goes down to the river to look. So far as river scenery
is concerned the barge might be at anchor. Even the motion of
the water is conceived of as devotedly attached to the boat. But

---

[26] *Henry VI, First Part,* I, i, 3-5.
[27] *Harold,* I, i, 66-72; I, ii, 263 *passim;* III, i, 203; v, i, 216.

in Tennyson the diamond ripples are at the bow, and regal
gardens are passed in review, while flocks of swans and the incoming tide distract attention from the purple throne of Pole.
These details are all interesting, orderly, and beautiful.   The
picture is a unity, but not a vital, warm, absorbing unity.   In
a somewhat similar way the scripture allusions in Tennyson's
dramas are effectively and happily made and are rich and
varied, yet do not in themselves point strongly in any one
direction, or climb, as they do in Shakespeare to any one climax.   The comparisons just made are very general.   They are
intended to point a direction, or create an atmosphere thru
which to see more sharply outlined and definite differences
between the two dramatists' use of the Bible.   It is hoped that
these specific differences may, to some extent at least, illuminate
the general character of Tennyson's dramatic work.   In the following pages Shakespeare's employment of Scripture is studied
in detail and after that Tennyson's method as seen in his three
long dramas.

SHAKESPEARE'S USE OF SCRIPTURE.

Shakespeare uses Scripture in its primary, literal, and natural
sense.   But he never enters into a scripture scene or story with
imaginative and elaborative delight, as Tennyson did in his first
period.   He uses one passage at a time for direct and imme-
diate effect.   This is true even where he employs two citations
in close connection.   Carlisle tells the assembled lords that if
they give the crown to Hereford,

> Disorder, horror, fear and mutiny
> Shall here inhabit, and this land be call'd
> The field of Golgotha and dead men's skulls.
> Oh! if you rear this house against this house,
> It will the woefullest division prove
> That ever fell upon this cursed earth.[28]

But the reference to Golgotha vivifies the conception of dis-
order and death, and the reference to the divided house enforces

---

[28] *Richard Second*, IV, i, 142-147; *Matthew*, XXVII, 33; XII, 25.

another and different idea, the evil of family conflict and civil war. Again, Richard urges, against giving up the crown, the fact that Northumberland's own record is

Mark'd with a blot, damn'd in the book of heaven [29]

and then in a moment adds

Though some of you with Pilate wash your hands,
Showing an outward pity; yet you Pilates
Have here deliver'd me to my sour cross,
And water cannot wash away your sin.[30]

But the book of heaven is connected with Northumberland's inconsistency, and Pilate's washing his hands with the fact that mere outward pity and ceremony cannot excuse an accompanying and deliberate sin. Combinations like those just cited are rare in Shakespeare, and even these have little or nothing in common with the combining method observed in Tennyson's second period. The difference appears at once when we compare them with Enoch's biblical speech to Annie, the mine promoter's interweavings in *Sea Dreams* or, to make a citation from the dramas, the dying words of King Edward.[31]

The fact that Shakespeare cites only one passage at a time of course precludes his fashioning and altering a set of scripture phrases into the forms necessary to build them into an allegory unified by some extra-scriptural conception like that of Humility in the *Holy Grail*. His simplicity and directness in making biblical allusions render such complex moulding still more impossible than piecing Scripture together into mosaics. In fact he seems never consciously and purposely to use scripture expressions, as Tennyson so often does, simply for the sake of their forceful idiom, their general biblical flavor, or their mere homogeneity with some general figure he happens to be using. It is the essential meaning, the straightforward, commonly accepted meaning, that he always has in mind. Even his satire makes more direct and obvious thrusts, tho sometimes

---

[29] *Richard Second*, IV, i, 236; *Psalms*, LIX, 28.
[30] *Richard Second*, IV, i, 239-242; *Matthew*, XXVII, 24.
[31] For the citations see pp. 38, 40, 66.

less powerful ones, than Tennyson's. Occasionally, as has already appeared in this study, Tennyson's reference is doubtful. Shakespeare's on the other hand is always unquestionable. It is never necessary to look it up or study its context.

It is not to be inferred from what has been said of Shakespeare's simplicity that he does not sometimes handle single passages of Scripture with great imaginative power. It is only contended that he uses but one passage at a time. Fairness perhaps requires that some illustrations of his genius in employing biblical citations be given at this point. The following are taken from *Macbeth* and *Hamlet* as examples from the tragedies and from *Measure for Measure* as from one of the comedies. Macduff knows that Duncan, as a King, is the Lord's anointed and that man's body is a sacred temple and says of the murdered King:

> Most sacriligious murder hath broke ope
> The Lord's anointed temple, and stole thence
> The life o' the building.[32]

When Macbeth falls into his last, fierce pessimism, he sees life as a place for fools, unrealities, and stage effects. The Psalmist said, " Our days on the earth are as a shadow " and again, " We spend our years as a tale that is told." Macbeth makes the shadow walk and puts the tale into the mouth of an imbecile:

> Life's but a walking shadow, a poor player
> That struts and frets his hour upon the stage,
> And then is heard no more; it is a tale
> Told by idiot, full of sound and fury,
> Signifying nothing.[33]

In the mature and finished *Hamlet* the scripture allusions are more numerous and of wider range. Two citations illustrate the extremes. The king's guilt forces him to say

> It hath the primal eldest curse upon't;
> A brother's murder.[34]

---

[32] *Macbeth*, II, iii, 67-69; *1 Corinthians*, III, 16, 17.
[33] *Macbeth*, V, v, 24-28; *Psalms*, CXLIV, 4 and XC, 9.
[34] *Hamlet*, III, iii, 37 f.; *Genesis*, IV, 11.

The First Clown can prove that Adam belonged to the nobility.

> *First Clown.* There is no ancient gentlemen but gardeners, ditchers, and grave-makers; they hold up Adam's profession.
> *Second Clown.* Was he a gentleman?
> *First Clown.* A' was the first that ever bore arms.
> *Second Clown.* Why he had none.
> *First Clown.* What! art a heathen? How dost thou understand the Scripture? The Scripture says, Adam digged; could he dig without arms? [35]

In *Measure for Measure* there is a reference to letting our light shine.

> Heaven doth with us as we with torches do,
> Not light them for ourselves; for if our virtues
> Did not go forth of us, 'twere all alike
> As if we had them not. Spirits are not finely touched
> But to fine issues.[36]

The commandment scraped out of the table which the pirate took with him when he went to sea may also be cited.[37] A complete examination of Shakespeare's dramas yields the conclusion that his rhetorical and literary power with Scripture is exercised upon isolated passages as distinguished from Tennyson's artistic blendings of many passages. Thruout his career Shakespeare's method was essentially the same; but Tennyson's was varied because of the stages of develpoment thru which it passed. Shakespeare always touched a passage briefly, naturally, and livingly; Tennyson often wrought one out more elaborately, and sometimes left upon it the mark of the chisel or the smell of the lamp.

There are at least four plays of Shakespeare which point a contrast of another kind. In each of these four the scripture citations are nearly all put into the mouth of the principal character in the play, or into the mouths of those who describe the qualities or career of that character. The citations are in close sympathy with the movement of the play and as a whole have an ethical intent. They point the moral as it were of

---

[35] *Hamlet*, v, i, 30-38; *Genesis*, II, 15.
[36] *Measure for Measure*, I, i, 32-36; *Matthew*, v, 14, 16.
[37] *Measure for Measure*, I, ii, 7-14; *Exodus*, xx, 15.

the successive situations and, as already intimated, reach at the
close of the drama a climax which pronounces a final moral
judgment on the whole action, or on the fate of the leading
character.   In subsequent pages of this study it will appear
that Tennysons' dramas employ Scripture with no such progressive and general ethical intent, but solely for its incidental
artistic help in portraying the various characters themselves.
Hence it may be, and in fact is, woven into the speeches of more
than one character in the same play.   The Scripture does not
play the part of an ethical standard, but that of a constantly
helpful and powerful artistic assistant.

The four plays referred to above are *Richard Second, Henry
Fourth, Richard Third,* and the *Merchant of Venice.*   Richard
II was fashioned for failure, for speech-making rather than
action.   By contrast, Bolingbroke was forceful and successful
even if unlovable.   The sequence of scripture allusions shows
the progress of the contrasted success and failure together with
Shakespeare's special sympathy for Richard, the principal character portrayed.   In Gloucester's death Bolingbroke hears a
summons to active vengeance.   His blood

> like sacrificing Abel's, cries
> Even from the tongueless caverns of the earth
> To me for justice and rough chastisement;
> And, by the glorious worth of my descent,
> This arm shall do it or this life be spent.[38]

Bolingbroke and Mowbray insist upon a bloody conflict with
each other.   Richard seeks to stop the deadly quarrel.   He and
Mowbray make out of Jeremiah's simile a piece of rhetoric
that illustrates Richard's speechmaking inefficiency at the very
outset.

> *King Richard.*   Rage must be withstood
>   Give me his gage: lions make leopards tame.
> *Mowbray.*   Yea, but not change his spots.[39]

---

[38] *Richard Second,* I, i, 104-108; *Genesis,* IV, 4, 10.
[39] *Richard Second,* I, i, 173-175; *Jeremiah,* XIII, 23.

In the second act Isaiah furnishes Salisbury with the image of Richard's ruin.

> Ah, Richard, with the eyes of heavy mind
> I see thy glory like a shooting star
> Fall to the base earth from the firmament.[40]

From this point onward Richard himself describes the treacheries and hypocrisies that work his ruin. He hears that Bagot, Bushy, and Green have made peace with Bolingbroke and cries:

> O villains, vipers, damn'd without redemption,
> Dogs, easily won to fawn on any man!
> Snakes in my heart-blood warm'd, that sting my heart!
> Three Judases, each one thrice worse than Judas!
> Would they make peace? terrible hell make war
> Upon their spotted souls for this offence.[41]

In a passage already quoted Carlisle likens the land to Golgotha and the kingdom to a divided house.[42] A little further on Richard's sense of treachery makes bitter capital out of the betrayal of Jesus.

> I well remember
> The favors of these men; were they not mine?
> Did they not sometime cry, ' all hail ' to me?
> So Judas did to Christ: but he, in twelve,
> Found truth in all but one; I in twelve thousand, none.[43]

Again the action progresses from the betrayal to the self-excusing, seeming-pitiful but selfish and murderous judgment Richard's energetic enemies pronounce upon him. They are like the cold unscrupulous Roman governor in the gospel.[44] Still later Richard is required to read the accusing paper before he is deposed and exclaims

> Fiend, thou torment'st me ere I come to hell.[45]

His sentimental double-mindedness sets the Bible itself in antithesis to the Bible.

---

[40] *Richard Second*, II, iv, 18-20; *Isaiah*, XIV, 12.
[41] *Richard Second*, III, ii, 129-134; *Matthew*, XXVI, 14-16.
[42] See page 74.
[43] *Richard Second*, IV, i, 167-171; *Matthew*, XXVI, 49; *John*, XVII, 12.
[44] For the passage see page 75.
[45] *Richard Second*, IV, i, 270; *Matthew*, VIII, 29.

> As thus: ' come, little ones '; and then again,
> ' It is as hard to come as for a camel
> To thread the postern of a needle's eye.' [46]

At the prison-assassination Shakespeare's sympathy assigns the king the fierce and powerful courage of despair. He kills two of his murderers and as a scripture counterpart assigns them to the fire that is not quenched, and then gives a grand turn to the ancient verse regarding the return of the dust to earth and of the spirit to God who gave it:

> That hand shall burn in never quenching fire
> That staggers thus my person. Exton, thy fierce hand
> Hath with the king's blood stain'd the king's own land,
> Mount, mount my soul! thy seat is up on high,
> Whilst my gross flesh sinks downward, here to die. [47]

Then comes the final scripture judgment upon the murderers of Richard and, by implication, upon Bolingbroke himself:

> Though I did wish him dead,
> I hate the murderer, love him murdered.
> The guilt of conscience take thou for thy labor,
> But neither my good word nor princely favor:
> With Cain go wander through the shade of night. [48]

In both parts of *Henry Fourth* and in *The Merry Wives of Windsor* it is Falstaff who knows his Bible. He is poor as Job but not so patient.[49] He is not afraid of Goliath with a weaver's beam because life itself is a swift-moving shuttle.[50] He surely knows by experience the story of the prodigal.[51] If Adam fell in the state of innocency, what should poor Jack Falstaff do in the days of villainy? He has more flesh than other men and therefore more frailty.[52] Sometimes he is guilty of leaving the fear of God on the left hand.[53] If however mere fat makes

---

[46] *Richard Second*, v, v, 15-17; *Matthew*, XI, 28; XIX, 24.

[47] *Richard Second*, v, v, 108-112; *Mark*, IX, 44; *Eccl.* XII, 7.

[48] *Richard Second*, v, vi, 39-43; *1 John*, III, 15; *Genesis*, v, 14.

[49] *Second Part Henry Fourth*, I, ii, 127; *James*, v, 11.

[50] *Merry Wives of Windsor*, v, i, 23, 24; *1 Samuel*, XVII, 7.

[51] *Second Part Henry Fourth*, II, i, 146; *Luke*, XV, 11 seq.

[52] *First Part Henry Fourth*, III, iii, 172-174; *Genesis*, III, 6; *Romans*, VII, 18.

[53] *Merry Wives of Windsor*, II, ii, 23; *Romans*, III, 18.

a man hated, Pharoah's lean kine are to be loved.[54] He and
Harry may repent, but it will not be in ashes and sackcloth,
but in new silk and old sack.[55] He has irreverent knowledge of Lazarus and the dogs that licked his sores,[56] and
of Dives burning in hell.[57] He understands that as he that
handles pitch is defiled, so the company a man keeps af-
fects his morals.[58] Henry's goodness comes from his association with him, for a tree is known by its fruit.[59] It is
God who gives men a spirit of persuasion.[60] Men themselves,
however, must rouse up fear and trembling.[61] If he has an
enemy the man is an Ahitophel.[62] If men are saved by merit,
no hole in hell is hot enough for him.[63] A man who has plenty
of gold-pieces is possessed of a legion of " angels." [64] Falstaff can even make sport of Paul's lofty injunction to owe no
man anything but love.[65] Sometimes, in fine, his scripture
quotations are themselves, like Mrs. Ford's scriptural remark
about him, quite unquotable.[66] Falstaff's whole character may
be known by the Scripture he uses and by the way he uses it.
But, once more, in the closing scripture citation Shakespeare
passes an unrelenting judgment upon the profane and surfeited
fool and jester whose character he has created. Falstaff comes
before the bar of a single passage and is found guilty. What
was his wild and wanton story, and what had Henry's pro-
tracted association with him been but a long light-headed
dream? Falstaff's tongue had most certainly walked thru

---

[54] *First Part Henry Fourth*, II, iv, 481-483; *Genesis*, XLI, 19 f.
[55] *Second Part Henry Fourth*, I, ii, 198-199; *Jonah*, III, 6.
[56] *First Part Henry Fourth*, IV, ii, 25, 26; *Luke*, XVI, 20 f.
[57] *First Part Henry Fourth*, III, iii, 33, 34; *Luke*, XVI, 23 f.
[58] *First Part Henry Fourth*, II, iv, 421-423; *Ecclesiasticus*, XIII, 1.
[59] *First Part Henry Fourth*, II, iv, 436-438; *Matthew*, XII, 33.
[60] *First Part Henry Fourth*, I, ii, 152; *1 Kings*, XXII, 21.
[61] *Second Part Henry Fourth*, IV, iii, 14; *Philippians*, II, 12.
[62] *Second Part Henry Fourth*, I, ii, 35; *2 Samuel*, XV, 31.
[63] *First Part Henry Fourth*, I, ii, 109 f.; *James*, II, 24; *Luke*, XVI, 23 f.
[64] *Merry Wives of Windsor*, I, iii, 54; *Mark*, V, 9.
[65] *First Part Henry Fourth*, III, iii, 144; *Romans*, XIII, 8.
[66] *Merry Wives of Windsor*, II, i, 60-67; *Jonah*, II, 10.

the earth, and his eyes had stood out with fatness. But of such
the Psalmist had already said, " As a dream when one awaketh,
so, O Lord, when thou awakest thou wilt despise their image."

> I have long dreamed of such a kind of man,
> So surfeit-swell'd, so old, and so profane;
> But, being awaked, I do despise my dream.[67]

So Henry feels, and as Falstaff's unlimited wit at the expense
of Scripture is preceded by Shakespeare's most heartfelt reference to Jesus and his cross,[68] so it is also followed by this vision
of judgment.

Richard III is a man of fixed craftiness, unconquerable
force, and consistent devotion to the most satanic evil. His
murders and his own words show that he is " determined to
prove a villain." His use of Scripture constitutes equally
cogent evidence. It is as perverted as that of the amended Vivi-
en and far more extended and varied. Perversion of the Bible
is in fact an integral part of his adopted profession of evil.
He prays for God's pardon for Clarence's persecutors. It is
the Christian's part to pray for the wrong-doer, not to curse him.
To have cursed the prospective murderer, moreover, would
have been to curse himself.[69] He tells how men urge him to be
revenged on Rivers, Grey, and Vaughan and then soliloquises:

> But then I sigh, and, with a piece of scripture,
> Tell them that God bids us do good for evil:
> And thus I clothe my naked villainy
> With odd old ends stolen forth of holy writ,
> And seem a saint when most I play the devil.[70]

There is nothing like this in all the vast bulk of Scripture in
Tennyson's dramas. His evil characters pervert the sacred
words incidentally and temporarily. Perversion is not their
profession as it is with Richard. Of the two children smoth-
ered to death in the tower he says,

---

[67] *Second Part Henry Fourth*, v, v, 51-53; *Psalms*, LXXIII, 7-9 and esp. 20.
[68] *First Part Henry Fourth*, I, i, 24-27.
[69] *Richard Third*, I, iii, 315-319; *Luke*, VI, 27 f.
[70] *Richard Third*, I, iii, 334-338; *Romans*, XII, 17, 21; *2 Corinthians*,
XI, 14 f.

The Sons of Edward sleep in Abraham's bosom.[71]

When Queen Elizabeth and the Duchess of York upbraid him for his murders he calls for music to drown out such blasphemy.

> A flourish, trumpets! strike alarum, drums!
> Let not the heavens hear these tell-tale women
> Rail on the Lord's anointed. Strike, I say.[72]

He asks Elizabeth to press his suit upon her daughter. His heart is pure, immaculate, devoted. Elizabeth replies and he retorts:

> *Queen Elizabeth.* Shall I be tempted of the devil thus?
> *King Richard.* Aye, if the devil tempt thee to do good.[73]

And finally, in a passage already alluded to in another connection, he perverts the shining of the sun of God's universal love in favor of his evil life. Does not God cause his light to fall on the evil as well as the good?

> Not shine today! Why, what is that to me
> More than to Richmond? For the selfsame heaven
> That frowns on me looks sadly upon him.[74]

Just before the end comes the one unperverted allusion. The thousand-tongued witness of a self-accusing and self-condemning conscience pronounces its sentence upon Richard's whole career.

> My conscience hath a thousand several tongues,
> And every tongue brings in a several tale
> And every tale condemns me for a villain.[75]

In the *Merchant of Venice* a very different biblical vein is worked. Shylock is familiar with the *New Testament* as well as with the *Old*. He will not dine with Bassanio lest there be pork on the table. He recalls the swine of Gadara and will not "eat of the habitation which your prophet the Nazarite con-

---

[71] *Richard Third,* IV, iii, 38; *Luke,* XVI, 22.
[72] *Richard Third,* IV, iv, 149-151; *Psalms,* II, 2.
[73] *Richard Third,* IV, iv, 419 f.; *Matthew,* IV, 1 seq.
[74] *Richard Third,* V, iii, 286-288; *Matthew,* V, 45.
[75] *Richard Third,* V, iii, 194-196; *Romans,* II, 15.

jured the devil into." [76]   Any Christian looks to him like a
fawning publican. [77]   He defends his usury by a full account
of Jacob's methods with Laban's flocks. [78]   He appeals to Father Abram [79] and swears by Jacob's staff [80] and by the holy
Sabbath. [81]   He calls Launcelot a fool of Hagar's offspring. [82]
He is aware of God's curse upon his nation but never really felt
it till he lost the costly diamond. [83]   Then comes the resolving
incident of the " Daniel come to judgment," the " second Daniel," and " still the Second Daniel." [84]   Then, once more, at
the end, as in *Richard Second,* occurs a double scripture climax
which sets the silent music of the spheres [85] against the noisy
disharmonies of earth, and sets Shylock's greed and murderous
hate against the kindly deeds of those who let their good light
shine forth among men.

> That light you see is burning in my hall,
> How far that little candle throws his beams!
> So shines a good deed in a naughty world. [86]

In Shakespeare, then, the scripture passages are employed
in the interest of manifest destiny, dramatic development, or
the verdict of conscience.   Taken all together and in their
climax the citations give the moral of the play.   They are for
the most part connected with a single character and progress
to a final ethical judgment upon him.   In contrast to this
extended and continuous ethical purpose, the use of Scripture
in Tennyson's dramas, though far more frequent, is nevertheless incidental and temporary.   It is a vehicle for single and
local expressions.   It may therefore be, and it actually is,

[76] *Merchant of Venice,* I, iii, 32 f.; *Matthew,* VIII, 31 f.
[77] *Merchant of Venice,* I, iii, 39; *Luke,* XVIII, 11.
[78] *Merchant of Venice,* I, iii, 75-88; *Genesis,* XXX, 31-43.
[79] *Merchant of Venice,* I, iii, 158; *John,* VIII, 53.
[80] *Merchant of Venice,* II, v, 36; *Genesis,* XXXII, 10.
[81] *Merchant of Venice,* IV, i, 36; *Exodus,* XX, 8.
[82] *Merchant of Venice,* II, v, 43; *Genesis,* XVI, 16.
[83] *Merchant of Venice,* III, i, 82-84; *Malachi,* III, 9.
[84] *Merchant of Venice,* IV, i, 221, 332, 339; *Daniel,* IV, 8.
[85] *Merchant of Venice,* V, i, 60-65; *Psalms,* XIX, 2-4.
[86] *Merchant of Venice,* V, i, 89-91; *Matthew,* V, 16.

wrought into the portrayal of more than one character in the same play. It is the constant, varied, and striking artistic fitness with which Tennyson can use the Scriptures in portraying any outstanding character that constitutes the richness and greatness of his employment of it in the dramas. Every such character makes many fine uses of single passages. But the unity of all the passages so used is the unity of constant artistic fitness rather than of general dramatic or ethical movement. The details of this use in the three great dramas will now be noted. The shorter ones may be omitted, for they are nearly scriptureless. There are no biblical references in *The Falcon* unless it be to the prodigal son (line 102), none in *The Cup* unless it be the " accuse and excuse " (ii, 67; compare *Romans*, ii, 15). In any case the play is based on Plutarch and is classic. *The Promise of May* has forgiveness for its theme, but does not refer in any outstanding way to anything except the " seventy times seven " (iii, 7-9; compare *Matthew*, xviii, 22, 35).

Queen Mary

In Queen Mary no less than five of the *dramatis personae* use biblical passages in a manner which effectively reveals the character and condition of each. Gardiner is a brutal and heavy-minded opportunist who does the work of a Spanish Inquisitor with British directness and outspoken scorn. He uses enough Scripture to show all these qualities. He comes with the royal procession to the newly decorated conduit and finds " Word of God " inscribed upon it in English. This he orders painted out, tho with impotent imagination he can think only of a pair of gloves to take its place.[87] Then a moment later he rages at the attendant:

> Word of God
> In English! over this the brainless loons
> That cannot spell Esaias from Saint Paul,
> Make themselves drunk and mad, fly out and flare

---

[87] *Queen Mary*, iii, i, 156-163; *Romans*, x, 17.

> Into rebellions. I'll have their Bibles burnt.
> The Bible is the priest's.[88]

He has an altercation with Paget before Queen Mary. He urges the most remorseless persecutions by burning at the stake. Tennyson's combining skill with Scripture enables him to do this in allusions to the New Testament.

> There must be heat—there must be heat enough
> To scorch and wither heresy to the root.
> For what saith Christ? 'Compel them to come in.'
> And what saith Paul? 'I would they were cut off
> That trouble you.' Let the dead letter live! [89]

Paget tells him he found

> One day a wholesome scripture, 'Little children,
> Love one another.'

But Gardiner retorts,

> Did you find a scripture,
> 'I come not to bring peace but a sword'? The sword
> Is in her Grace's hand to smite with.[90]

When Pole accuses him of denying the Holy Father in the days of Henry VIII, he defends his ecclesiastical shifting with shameless readiness.

> even Saint Peter in his time of fear
> Denied his Master, ay, and thrice, my lord.[91]

A moment later he asks Bonner whether he would not be glad to revenge himself upon the heretics for imprisoning him.

> Would'st thou not burn and blast them root and branch? [92]

And finally when he is alone with Bonner he reaffirms his policy "to dodge, or duck, or die." For the present he will

---

[88] *Queen Mary*, III, i, 166-171; *Romans*, IX, 16 f.
[89] *Queen Mary*, III, iv, 16-20; *Luke*, XIV, 23; *Galatians*, v, 12; *2 Corinthians*, III, 6.
[90] *Queen Mary*, III, iv, 54-57; *1 John*, III, 18; *Matthew*, X, 34.
[91] *Queen Mary*, III, iv, 165 f.; *Matthew*, XXVI, 69-74.
[92] *Queen Mary*, III, iv, 176; *Malachi*, IV, 1.

favor the Pope's deadly statutes and thus assist that mighty slave of slaves to "plunge his foreign fist into our island church,"

> And that his fan may thoroughly purge his floor.[93]

In rendering the character of Cole, the canting Catholic priest who delights in killing a great protestant, Tennyson again reveals his long-time skill in combining scripture passages, together with his later acquisition of strength in scriptural satire. The scene is in Saint Mary's church. The choir breaks forth into the *Nunc Dimittis*. Cole is in the pulpit. Cranmer is conspicuously set upon a scaffold. Cole preaches at Cranmer and to the people. He stands like a carrion-crow watching a sick beast before it dies. He expresses sympathy in the language of Paul. Then, all unconsciously, he uses the language of his prototype, Caiaphas, the murderous Sadducee.

> Weep with him if ye will,
> Yet—
> It is expedient for one man to die,
> Yea, for the people, lest the people die.[94]

He assures the murmuring Protestants that, notwithstanding his repentance, Cranmer must burn, that all

> May learn there is no power against the Lord.[95]

Then comes the sickening but strong passage in which are gathered and blended the poet's artistic powers with Scripture, seen separately in the periods of combination, allegory, and satire. Even the facility in adding legend to Scripture in order to secure a larger homogeneous bulk of reference is not absent:

> Yet, Cranmer, be thou glad.
> This is the work of God. He is glorified
> In thy conversion; lo! thou art reclaim'd;
> He brings thee home; nor fear but that today
> Thou shalt receive the penitent thief's award,

---

[93] *Queen Mary*, III, iv, 227; *Matthew*, III, 12.
[94] *Queen Mary*, IV, iii, 9-12; *Romans*, XII, 15; *John*, XI, 50.
[95] *Queen Mary*, IV, iii, 43; *Proverbs*, XXI, 30.

> And be with Christ the Lord in Paradise.
> Remember how God made the fierce fire seem
> To those three children like a pleasant dew.
> Remember, too,
> The triumph of Saint Andrew on his cross,
> The patience of Saint Lawrence in the fire.[96]

Surely Tennyson's art with Scripture in this passage has fastened Cole to his pedestal of infamy more securely than anything in prose history has done.

After Caiaphas-Cole with his callous caricature of vicarious sacrifice may be placed Cranmer himself.' He cites the Mosaic law in defense of his work for the divorce of Catherine,

> 'Thou shalt not wed thy brother's wife.'—'Tis written,
> 'They shall be childless.' [97]

The picture of his last hours is highly effective. He is in prison at Oxford.

> Last night, I dreamed the faggots were alight,
> And that myself was fasten'd to the stake,
> And found it all a visionary flame,
> Cool as the light in old decaying wood;
> And then King Harry look'd from out a cloud,
> And bade me have good courage; and I heard
> An angel cry, 'There is more joy in heaven,'—
> And after that the trumpet of the dead.[98]

These dream-citations finely anticipate and illustrate the martyr's actual repentance and inward resurrection. His last speech is a tissue of scripture citations, adaptations, interweavings, and combinations and breathes thruout the spirit of a meek and heroic calm. It contains separate and distinct echoes of the sayings of the psalmist, the prodigal, and the publican, of Isaiah, John, Paul, Peter, and James. There are perhaps a score of clear allusions, but they are so finely and effectively altered as to be understood only by reading the whole

---

[96] *Queen Mary*, IV, iii, 54-64; *Galatians*, I, 24; *Luke*, XXIII, 43; *Daniel*, IV, 20-28; *Luke*, VI, 14.

[97] *Queen Mary*, I, ii, 40 f.; *Leviticus*, XX, 21.

[98] *Queen Mary*, IV, ii, 1-9; *Luke*, XV, 7; *1 Corinthians*, XV, 52.

passage. It is too long to quote here. Cranmer confesses like the prodigal and feels his helplessness like David and Isaiah. He knows that for great sins like his Christ was made flesh and died, and that God the Father gave Him up to death. He laments men's love of the world, which is hatred against God. He recognizes even the persecuting Mary and Philip as God's ministers. He urges men to live together like brethren and as far as in them lieth to do good to all. He reminds the rich of how hard it is to enter the Kingdom of God, and urges men to deeds of charity because Christ is with us in the poor.[99]

To the brutal citations of Gardiner, the cantish citations of Cole, and the gentle citations of Cranmer, may be added the nice and pretty citations of Pole, the accomplished cardinal and papal legate to Mary's court. He hails Mary in scripture Latin.[100] He tells how the shores of the Thames wore in his eyes the green of Paradise.[101] He had had an attack of dizziness in Flanders but

> The scarlet thread of Rahab saved her life;
> And mine, a little letting of the blood.[102]

His native land had marked him even as Cain, yet he returns as Peter but to bless her.[103] He very prettily tells Mary how when Peter knocked at her gate she herself like the apostolic Mary would have been glad to have risen and let him in.[104] Then he gives her some more biblical Latin.[105] When she is sitting between Philip and himself he tells her she is enclosed with boards of cedar, "our little sister of the Song of Songs."[106]

---

[99] *Queen Mary*, IV, iii, 77-152; *Luke*, XV, 18, 21; *Isaiah*, XX, 6; X, 3; *Luke*, XVIII, 13; *Romans*, III, 6; *John*, VI, 37; I, 14; *1 Timothy*, III, 16; *John*, III, 16; *Matthew*, XII, 32; *John*, XVII, 1 f.; *James*, IV, 4; *1 John*, II, 15; *1 Peter*, II, 13 f.; *Romans*, XIII, 4; *Galatians*, VI, 10; *1 John*, IV, 16, 20; *Matthew*, XIX, 23; *Proverbs*, XIX, 17.

[100] *Queen Mary*, III, ii, 1; *Luke*, I, 28.

[101] *Queen Mary*, III, ii, 10 f.; *Luke*, XXIII, 43.

[102] *Queen Mary*, III, ii, 23 f.; *Joshua*, II, 18; VI, 17.

[103] *Queen Mary*, III, ii, 34 f.; *Genesis*, IV, 15.

[104] *Queen Mary*, III, ii, 39-42; *Acts*, XII, 11-17.

[105] *Queen Mary*, III, ii, 52; *Luke*, I, 42.

[106] *Queen Mary*, III, ii, 62 f.; *Song of Solomon*, VIII, 8 f.

In the great hall in Whitehall, when parliament makes its humble submission to the King and Queen and prays them to intercede with the apostolic see for their absolution, he thinks that all the breath of England should rise to the heavens in grateful praise.[107]   The blessed gospel angels who rejoice over one that is saved [108] triumph in the re-born salvation of the land.   By giving them absolution he renders them thanks more than any earthly field does for being sowed.   He gives sixty-fold, a hundred, yea, a thousand-thousand fold.[109]   Finally he rises and gives his benediction in a neat and graceful scripture complication:

> The Lord who hath redeem'd us
> With His own blood, and washed us from our sins,
> To purchase for Himself a stainless bride;
> He, whom the Father hath appointed Head
> Of all his church, He by His mercy absolve you.[110]

Pole desires to delay persecution in the hope that the church may win outsiders by her attractiveness,

> When she once more is seen
> White as the light, the spotless bride of Christ,
> Like Christ Himself on Tabor.[111]

Even when at last he is cited to Rome to answer for heresy before the Inquisition his final scriptural phrases are graceful in their sentimental sadness:

> it was thought we two
> Might make one flesh, and cleave unto each other
> As man and wife
>
> .   .   .   .
>
> No—we were not made
> One flesh in happiness, no happiness here;
> But now we are made one flesh in misery;
> Our bridesmaids are not lovely—Disappointment,

---

[107] *Queen Mary*, III, iii, 103 f.; *Psalms*, CXLI, 2.

[108] *Queen Mary*, III, iii, 114-116; *Luke*, XV, 10.

[109] *Queen Mary*, III, iii, 129-132; *Matthew*, XIII, 8.

[110] *Queen Mary*, III, iii, 132-136; *Revelation*, V, 9; I, 5; XIX, 7; *Ephesians*, V, 23.

[111] *Queen Mary*, III, iv, 124-126; *Ephesians*, V, 27; *Matthew*, XVII, 2.

Ingratitude, Injustice, Evil-tongue,
Labor-in-vain.[112]

The references which Mary herself makes to Scripture are somewhat numerous. They are threaded on the heartstring of her passion for Philip. If she can have him she will for his sake restore the Roman Church in England.

Give me my Philip; and we two will lead
The living waters of the Faith again
Back thro' their widow'd channel here, and watch
The parch'd banks rolling incense, as of old,
To heaven, and kindled with the palms of Christ! [113]

It is for Philip's sake that she desires her child,

if it might please God that I should leave
Some fruit of mine own body after me.[114]

It is her love for him that inspires her peculiar scripture rhapsody,

He hath awaked! He hath awaked!
He stirs within the darkness!
O Philip, husband! now thy love to mine
Will cling more close, and those bleak manners thaw,
That make me shamed and tongue-tied in my love.
The second Prince of Peace—
The great unborn defender of the Faith,
Who will avenge me of mine enemies—
He comes, and my star rises.

. . . . . .
His sceptre shall go forth from Ind to Ind!
. . . .
                                    Open
Ye everlasting gates! The King is here!—
My star, my son! [115]

But at the end her illusion breaks completely. She knows Philip hates her and desires her death. Music may give her a little comfort.

[112] *Queen Mary*, v, ii, 81-83, 88-93; *Genesis*, ii, 24; *1 Corinthians*, xv, 58.
[113] *Queen Mary*, i, v, 57-61; *John*, iv, 10; xii, 13.
[114] *Queen Mary*, ii, ii, 142 f.; *Psalms*, cxxxii, 11.
[115] *Queen Mary*, iii, ii, 92-100, 109, 112-114; *Isaiah*, ix, 6; i, 24; *Numbers*, xxiv, 17; *Psalms*, xxiv, 7.

> They say the gloom of Saul
> Was lighten'd by young David's harp.[116]

She takes the lute and sings her song with its exquisite refrain " Low, dear lute, low." But the lute's key is not low enough. The maid's compliment on her low voice angers her, for Philip does not like her low voice. " Even for that he hates me." To all this Tennyson's art with Scripture finds a profound climax in *Isaiah.* Yes, her voice is low. It is as if she were already dead and her ghost were speaking from the grave:

> A low voice from the dust and from the grave! [117]

Later on she sends her grim disenchanted message to Philip. It is not an heir, but death, that is coming. The practical apostle furnishes her the satiric figure,

> Tell him at last I know his love is dead,
> And that I am in state to bring forth death.[118]

Even in the very hour of death Philip still rules her thought. Her mind wanders scripturally. She has been too slack with heretics. She must do more burning at once,

> We'll follow Philip's leading, and set up
> The Holy Office here—garner the wheat,
> And burn the tares with unquenchable fire! [119]

Before passing to the examination of *Harold* and *Becket* a few general remarks may be made. Their truth is evident from *Queen Mary,* and the two later dramas will serve to make it clearer still. How strong a testimony it is to the combined mastery which Tennyson in these later years has over Scripture that Mary's uses of biblical language, even if taken separately in their closest connections, give us all the stages of her passion. Its rise and ripening, its power to make her persecute, and its issue in disappointment and death are all

[116] *Queen Mary,* v, ii, 205 f.; *1 Samuel,* xvi, 23.
[117] *Queen Mary,* v, ii, 222; *Isaiah,* xxix, 4.
[118] *Queen Mary,* v, ii, 335 f.; *James* i, 15.
[119] *Queen Mary,* v, v, 68-70; *Matthew,* xiii, 40.

clearly seen through the medium of phrases from the King James version. Yet even this testimony must be multiplied by five, for in this same drama the same vehicle carries, as has been shown, effective portrayals of four other characters as different from each other and from Mary as Gardiner, Cole, Cranmer, and Pole.

The difference between Tennyson's hand at Scripture and Shakespeare's is also made obvious. Tennyson's citations taken together constitute a progress to a climax of artistic description. But the progress and climax do not intrinsically or exclusively inhere in the scripture passages themselves. The Scripture furnishes artistic material which is blended with other material and used in common with it. It stands on the same footing with it. Shakespeare's references, on the contrary, have an independent moral worth and position. The climax they lead to is not an integral part of the climax of the action of the drama. In Shakespeare the citations sit outside the drama, as it were, upon the bench of conscience, and the closing one pronounces a final moral verdict. In a word, Tennyson's citations are primarily and mainly the product of artistic talent. In Shakespeare they are the product of conscience.

It may be asked whether Tennyson is true to realism in assigning to each of five separate characters in the same play a series of corresponding scripture passages. Shakespeare confines anything resembling such a strong and continuous usage to a single character. Nor is it artistically necessary that cardinals and bishops talk in biblical dialect. Shakespeare's Wolsey, for example, does not do so. Men in high ecclesiastical office, moreover, often scrupulously avoid scriptural language lest their words savor of professionalism. But, on the other hand, it may be fairly urged that Mary's reign was a time of great religious ferment. The question of the day may be put thus: " Shall the Bible be in Latin for the priests or in English for the people? " Bible-language was in men's hearts. Out of the abundance of the heart the mouths of the day might well speak.

To the foregoing remarks it may perhaps be added that
there is no better way of seeing the mastery and unity with
which Tennyson portrays any one main character in his dramas
than to follow it along the scripture pathway. In studying
the previous periods a similar advantage has appeared. The
way Tennyson used the Bible gave added clearness to the way
he used other material. The easy possibility of isolating his
method with Scripture casts light upon his method of using
other classes of material not so easily separable from one another. It is an analogous fact that the Scripture used by a character in a drama is so familiar that the individual passion and
mood into which it is cast are instinctively seen. Sufficient
passages are cited in the portrayal of each character to afford
a continuous line of stepping stones on which to pass thru the
entire drama. To change the figure, the scripture passages
keep the reader from losing his way amid the rich foliage of
the woods because so many trees are blazed that the trail is
clear. Or, to change the illustration once more, the way a
character uses Scripture furnishes a key to unlock the problem
of the general development of that character in the drama.

Harold.

In *Harold* King Edward is worthy of study because Tennyson evidently conceives of the Confessor's mind and tongue as
full of biblical phrases and images. He sees the flaming comet
in the sky and the gross, unlearned priests on earth and exclaims

> In heaven signs!
> Signs upon earth! Signs everywhere! [120]

His life has been pure. He has built the great church of Holy
Peter, Westminster Abbey. His end is near.

> I have fought the fight and go—
> I see the flashing of the gates of pearl—
> And it is well with me.[121]

---

[120] *Harold*, I, i, 85 f.; *Daniel*, VI, 27.
[121] *Harold*, I, i, 102-104; *2 Timothy*, IV, 7; *Revelation*, XXI, 21; *1 Kings*,
IV, 26.

On his sick-bed he sees his strange mystic vision of the green
tree with its echoes from *Luke,* the *Apocalypse,* the *Psalms,* and
Daniel allegorically moulded together to outline the destiny of
the English people.[122]   Then he starts up and describes in a
remarkable interweaving of verses the dedication of the great
church.[123]   Finally he expresses the curse that will result from
Harold's forswearing himself:

> Treble denial of the tongue of flesh,
> Like Peter's when he fell, and thou wilt have
> To wail for it like Peter.[124]

In effective contrast to the pietistic flavor of Edward's citations is the hearty and rough good sense of Harold himself.
Gamel is no rolling stone, but he has rounded since Harold
met him last.[125]   Wrecked on the shore at Ponthieu, Harold
accuses the fishermen there of being " wreckers ":

Harold.   Fishermen? devils!
Who, while ye fish for men with your false fires,
Let the great devil fish for your own souls.
  Rolf.   Nay then, we be liker the blessed apostles; they were fishers of
men, Father Jean says.
  Harold.   I had liefer that the fish had swallowed me,
Like Jonah, than have known there were such devils.[126]

After he had taken the forced oath, at Bayeux, to help William
to the crown of England, Malet thanks him for having saved
himself.   Harold replies with rough conscientiousness,

> For having lost myself to save myself.[127]

When he is alone with Wulfnoth his raging mind would have
the " earth rive, gulf in these cursed Normans," as it did Korah,
Dathan, and Abiram.[128]   With healthy mental vigor he laughs
the pope's anathema to scorn and reminds the horrified Edith

---

[122] *Harold*, III, i, 76-91; *Luke*, XXIII, 31; *Revelation*, XIV, 6; *Daniel*, IV, 20.
[123] *Harold*, III, i, 101-109.   (See for the passage in full, p. 66).
[124] *Harold*, III, i, 161-163; *Matthew*, XXVI, 69-75.
[125] *Harold*, I, i, 51 f.; *Ezra*, V, 8 margin.
[126] *Harold*, II, i, 17-24; *Matthew*, IV, 19; *Jonah*, I, 17.
[127] *Harold*, II, ii, 355; *Matthew*, X, 39.
[128] *Harold*, II, ii, 425 f.; *Numbers*, XVI, 32.

that the Roman emperors called themselves Gods just because
they were emperors and laughed at Jewish ecclesiastics who
questioned their divine right to tribute.   Jesus, the good shepherd, himself told men to yield obedience to the reigning power.
Popes make themselves objects of laughter by giving commands
different from their Lord's:

> This was old human laughter in old Rome
> Before a Pope was born, when that which reign'd
> Call'd itself God.—A kindly rendering
> Of ' Render unto Caesar '—The Good Shepherd!
> Take this, and render that.[129]

In the same vein Harold says that Christ was God and came
to earth as a man, whereas the Pope is man and comes as
God.[130]   When the Danes tell him he is not of kingly stock,
but only the grandson of Wulfnoth the poor cowherd, he takes
his stand on kingly qualities and boldly likens the poor cowherd
to Jesus, for he

> Had in him kingly thoughts—a king of men,
> Not made but born, like the great king of all,
> A light among the oxen.[131]

Referring to the fact that tho he loved Edith he married Ald-
wyth of Wales merely to gain Morcar's adherence, he says in
view of the ill-success of the measure,

> Evil for good, it seems,
> Is oft as childless of the good as evil
> For evil.[132]

In any case he must fight tomorrow and must have some sleep.

> A snatch of sleep were like the peace of God.
> . . . .
> Were the great trumpet blowing doomsday dawn,
> I needs must rest.[133]

---

[129] *Harold*, III, ii, 96-100; *2 Thessalonians*, II, 4; *Matthew*, XXII, 21; *John*,
X, 11.

[130] *Harold*, III, ii, 101 f.; *1 Corinthians*, XV, 47; *Philippians*, II, 8.

[131] *Harold*, IV, i, 46-48; *Luke*, II, 7.

[132] *Harold*, V, i, 98-100; *Romans*, III, 8; XII, 17.

[133] *Harold*, V, i, 103, 127 f.; *Philippians*, IV, 7; *1 Corinthians*, XV, 52.

The Bible can yield this man nothing but the counsel of hale and hearty common sense. It does yield him that and his use of it reveals his character.

BECKET.

In *Becket* King Henry's employment of Scripture strikes the consistent note of an absolute monarch. Becket affronts and defies the king with a spiritual power as unyielding as Henry's secular power. Henry chafes over this to the little child Geoffrey in Rosamund's bower:

> *Henry.* Dost thou know, my boy, what it is to be Chancellor of England?
> *Geoffrey.* Something good, or thou wouldst not give it me.
> *Henry.* It is, my boy, to side with the king when Chancellor, and then to be made archbishop and go against the king who made him, and turn the world upside down.
> *Geoffrey.* I won't have it then. Nay, but give it me, and I promise thee not to turn the world upside down.[134]

At Montmirail Henry meets Louis and Becket. He is half beside himself with passion and the Bible helps him to say the bitterest and ugliest possible things about Becket. He calls him one

> Who thief-like fled from his own church by night
> No man pursuing.[135]

The allusion makes Becket a thief, cowardly, and wicked. But the impassioned monarch does worse yet and classes his archbishop with senseless swine. He says of him to Louis,

> Take heed he do not turn and rend you, too.[136]

Then, a little later, Henry's absolutism deifies itself with a commandment,

> look you, you shall have
> None other God but me—me, Thomas, son
> Of Gilbert Becket, London merchant. Out!
> I hear no more.[137]

---

[134] *Becket*, II, i, 120-131; *Acts*, XVII, 6.
[135] *Becket*, II, ii, 87 f.; *Proverbs*, XXVIII, 1.
[136] *Becket*, II, ii, 89; *Matthew*, VII, 6.
[137] *Becket*, II, ii, 130-132; *Exodus*, XX, 3.

7

However, if Becket would submit, the king might even now, at
Fréteval, play the gracious God from whom all power comes.

> I might deliver all things to thy hand.[138]

In Walter Map, Tennyson has drawn a Scripture-using character radically different from any this study has yet shown in
his dramas. Falstaff and Map are morally antithetical. Falstaff uses Scripture for pure wantonness, jesting, and lying.
Map, at heart, is serious, honest, and helpful. Yet scripture
usage sometimes makes strange bedfellows. Falstaff would be
a character impossible for Tennyson on the ground of ethical
attitude alone. Yet somehow he is suggested by Map. Each
of the two talks in prose, each handles the Word with a kind of
irreverent and rollicking exaggeration, and each gives the impression of being able to go on indefinitely with his special kind
of performance. Falstaff and Map know their Bible equally
well. Examples of Falstaff's abilities in this matter have already been given.[139] Similar proofs of Map's are easily
afforded. He urges Becket to make peace with Henry.

> Agree
> With him quickly again, even for the sake of the Church.[140]

The omission of the " adversary," the " officer," and the " prison" gives the quotation the added force of vivid implication.
Of Henry's quickly altered attitude toward Becket, Map says
"Sudden change is a house on sand." [141] With a grotesque
turn he adds that Henry has " pulled all the Church with the
Holy Father astride of it down upon his own head.[142] At the
crowning of Henry's son, Salisbury looked to Map " like a thief
at night when he hears a door open in the house and thinks ' the
master.' " [143] After the crowning followed " the thunder of

---

[138] *Becket*, III, iii, 202; *John*, III, 35.
[139] See pages 80 f.
[140] *Becket*, II, ii, 234-236; *Matthew*, v, 25.
[141] *Becket*, III, iii, 41; *Matthew*, VII, 26 f.
[142] *Becket*, III, iii, 57-59; *Judges*, XVI, 30.
[143] *Becket*, III, iii, 78-80; *Matthew*, XXIV, 43.

the captains and the shouting." [144]   After that came the banquet.   "As to the fish, they de-miracled the miraculous draught, and might have sunk a navy."   "As for the flesh at table, a whole Peter's sheet, with all manner of game, and fourfooted things, and fowls—." [145]   Map's quality is perhaps evident without further citations.

It has been said that the key to Becket's problematical character was his passion for thoroness and that Tennyson has furnished that key.   Whatever Becket does he does with his whole soul.   He beats the king at chess because he gives his mind unreservedly to the game.   For the same reason while he is chancellor he defends the throne with his entire strength.   Feeling himself forced into the archbishopric by the conviction that he was born for it, by the death-bed desire of Theobald, and by Henry's insistence, he accepts the mitre.   But his thoroness in office digs a deep ravine between him and the king.   Henry is maddened and Becket is inflexible.   This conception of Tennyson's seems true to history.   But Becket's use of Scripture reveals a thoroness within the thoroness.   His devotion to the church, indeed, makes him bewail the low estate of

> Our holy mother Canterbury, who sits
> With tatter'd robes.[146]

At the Traitor's Meadow he combines phrases from the *Apocalypse, Isaiah,* and *2 Kings* with the same intent.[147] He is determined to restore the church to her power and her glory. But the completeness of his devotion to the church merges itself in a mystic union of himself with Christ as its head.   It is in the thoroness of that personal identification that the secret of Becket's ecclesiastical thoroness lies.   And the expression of the identification appears in scriptural allusions running thru the portrayal to the very end.   By following these an intenser conception of it is gained than in any other way.   It has the

---

[144] *Becket,* III, iii, 92-93; *Job,* XXXIX, 25.
[145] *Becket,* III, iii, 103-111; *Luke,* v, 6; *Acts,* x, 11.
[146] *Becket,* I, i, 90 f.; *Isaiah,* III, 26.
[147] *Becket,* III, iii, 150; *Revelation,* XXI, 9; *Isaiah,* I, 8; *2 Kings,* x, 19.

effect of walking over a long and lofty ridge from which the
great reaches of Becket's total inner landscape are widely
visible.   It is one thing to recognize the theory that an archbishop represents Christ.   It is another thing to produce an
artistic portrayal of the head of a church consistently and pas-
sionately living up to that theory.   Becket will not have the
cleric dragged before the civil judgment seat.   But the form
his protest takes is,

> The Lord be judged again by Pilate?   No! [148]

Again, when Leicester followed by barons and bishops demands
that Becket stand and hear his judgment sentence, Becket in-
terrupts,

> Judgment!   Barons!
> Who but the bridegroom dares to judge the bride,
> Or he the bridegroom may appoint?
>
> . . . .
>
> I charge thee, upon pain of mine anathema,
> That thou obey, not me, but God in me,
> Rather than Henry. [149]

When his retainers leave him Becket acts the part of the Lord
and makes the parable of the Great Supper his own appeal.
"Was not my lord of Leicester bidden to our supper. . . .
Shall God's good gifts be wasted?   None of them here!   Call
in the poor from the streets." [150]   To those who have deserted
him he says in evident appropriation of phrases used by Jesus,
"Ye have eaten of my dish and drunken of my cup for a dozen
years." [151]   At Montmirail the identification deepens.   Voices
from the crowd call out blessings upon the lord archbishop.   In
appropriating them Becket puts himself in the position of
Jesus at the Triumphal Entry when the crowd cried "Hosanna."

> Out of the mouths of babes and sucklings, praise!
> I thank you, sons. [152]

---

[148] *Becket*, I, iii, 59; *Matthew*, XXVII, 2.

[149] *Becket*, I, iii, 389-391, 408-410; *John*, III, 29.

[150] *Becket*, I, iv, 54 f., 67-69; *Luke*, XIV, 16-24.

[151] *Becket*, I, iv, 28 f.; *Matthew*, XX, 23; XXVI, 23.

[152] *Becket*, II, ii, 158 f.; *Psalms*, VIII, 2; *Matthew*, XXI, 16.

Again, and still at Montmirail, he represents Henry as Pilate, and himself as Christ,

> On mine own self
> The king had had no power except for Rome,
> 'Tis not the King who is guilty of mine exile,
> But Rome, Rome, Rome! [153]

Tempting Becket to meet Henry's conditions of power is tempting Christ, as in the wilderness, to fall down and worship the devil.[154] Herbert understands Becket's position perfectly when he adds at once that he, Herbert, would gladly fall down and worship him, Becket, because the latter has " trodden the winepress alone." Nor does Becket himself hesitate to continue the figure still further by saying " of the people there were many with me." [155] A little later still he makes himself a vicarious sacrifice for the Church, as a shepherd gives his life for his sheep. His death is as lonely as Christ's and works the same salvation:

> But I must die for that which never dies.
> It will be so—my visions in the Lord—
> It must be so, my friend! the wolves of England
> Must murder her one shepherd, that the sheep
> May feed in peace.[156]

Once more he identifies himself with Jesus before Pilate by saying to John of Salisbury at the close of his career that his " kingdom is not of this world." [157] And, once more also, he replies to Fitzurse's taunt that his return to England breaks the bonds of peace, by taking the position of Jesus at the Triumphal Entry. From the people at his return had come

> Sobs, laughter, cries; they spread their raiment down
> Before me.[158]

---

[153] *Becket*, II, ii, 257-260; *John*, XIX, 11.

[154] *Becket*, III, iii, 213 f.; *Matthew*, IV, 9.

[155] *Becket*, III, iii, 214-217; *Isaiah*, LXIII, 3.

[156] *Becket*, III, iii, 257-261; *2 Corinthians*, XII, 1; *Matthew*, XXVI, 31; *John*, X, 11, 15.

[157] *Becket*, V, ii, 10; *John*, XVIII, 36.

[158] *Becket*, V, ii, 199 f.; *Matthew*, XXI, 8.

To De Morville he assumes that in his work he is above all
mere men.

> I ask no leave of king, or mortal man.
> .   .   .   .   .   Alone I do it.
> Give to the King the things that are the King's,
> And those of God to God.[159]

These retorts of Becket seem, indeed, to have a somewhat proud,
and even boastful, tone.   But it must, in fairness, be noted
that, like Jesus on his last return to Jerusalem, Becket has come
back to England with the full, conscious, and clear-minded purpose of giving up his life.   He is

> Mail'd in the perfect panoply of faith,
> First of the foremost of their files who die
> For God, to people heaven in the great day
> When God makes up his jewels.[160]

Such a consecration almost requires a certain amount of self-
assertion, and Becket's character as a sacrifice is still further
emphasized when in the same scene John of Salisbury says
"They seek, you make,—occasion for your death " and Becket
replies,

> My counsel is already taken, John.
> I am prepared to die .   .   .   .
> God's will be done! [161]

In the last scene in the cathedral he is still the Lord's anointed.
The knights are battering at the doors.   " Why do the heathen
rage ? " [162]   At the very close of all, in the north transept, he
is not afraid of stumbling in the gloomy passages, for he goes
with steadfast feet because he is one with Jesus who knew that
his own hour which had come coincided with the hour and
power of darkness which had come to his enemies at last.

> Fear not I should stumble in the darkness,
> Not tho' it be their hour, the power of darkness,
> But my hour too, the power of light in darkness!

---

[159] *Becket*, v, ii, 247-250; *Matthew*, XXII, 21.
[160] *Becket*, v, ii, 267-270; *Ephesians*, VI, 13; *Malachi*, III, 17.
[161] *Becket*, v, ii, 305-309; *Mark*, XIV, 55; *Luke*, XX, 42.
[162] *Becket*, v, ii, 339; *Psalms*, II, 1.

> I am not in the darkness but the light,
> Seen by the Church in heaven, the Church on earth—
> The power of life in death to make her free! [163]

When the assassins lay hold of him he speaks as if he were
Jesus himself already risen from the dead. Tennyson means
to give Becket's words this meaning and De Brito is a right
interpreter when he connects Becket's " Touch me not " with
Jesus' words to Mary Magdalene at the open sepulchre.[164]
Wounded and staggering he falls to his knees, but in the very
article of death his last words are words of Jesus and his very
last word is the very last word on the Cross.

> At the right hand of Power—
> Power and great glory—for thy Church, O Lord—
> Into thy hands, O Lord—into thy hands! [165]

Clearly *Becket* is Tennyson's crowning triumph in the
artistic use of Scripture. It renews his earlier uses with no
small power. But it does more. In Becket himself Tennyson
has painted a high ecclesiastic who uses Scripture as a living
body to ensphere a great soul. Any ecclesiastic in any drama
is at liberty to make scripture allusions. It is entirely " in
character" to do so. But Tennyson's Becket plays the part
with a spiritual and dramatic unity and self-consistency and
with a continuous vital motion which no other dramatist has
equalled. We look in vain for any parallel in Shakespeare.
His ecclesiastics employ biblical allusions rarely. Winchester
does say

> Nay, stand thou back; I will not budge a foot.
> This be Damascus, be thou cursed Cain
> To slay thy brother Abel, if thou wilt.[166]

But Winchester has no other biblical allusions to go with this
one. In this feature Shakespeare approaches Tennyson near-
est in Shylock. Shylock, as was shown on an earlier page,[167]

---

[163] *Becket*, v, iii, 49-54; *Luke*, XXII, 53; *John*, XVII, 1.
[164] For the passage see p. 69.
[165] *Becket*, v, iii, 99-100; *Luke*, XXII, 69; XXIII, 46.
[166] *First Part, Henry VI*, I, iii, 38-40.
[167] See pages 83 f.

makes many allusions to both Testaments.   But the Bible is
a means of making the immortal Jew ludicrous and of covering
him with grotesque contempt.   Becket, as has been seen, takes
himself, and must be taken, with almost supernatural serious-
ness.   The account just given is necessarily imperfect.   For
Becket's references to Scripture are too numerous for complete
citation within the limits of these pages.   It is also to be
remembered that while it has been urged that the occurrences of
Scripture in this drama, if read in continuity and in isolation,
cast a helpful light upon the whole play, the converse proposition
is, of course, true also, and still more important.   The whole
drama must be read in order to feel the strength and beauty of
the biblical element it contains.

CHAPTER VI.

The Period of Disuse.

Completeness of treatment compels the recognition in Tennyson's use of Scripture of a sixth and final period. This may be termed the Period of Disuse. For aside from one or two historic references, the use of Scripture is now restricted to vague allusion. The thought is affected more than the art. In his first period Tennyson's poetry, as this study has shown, delighted in scripture scenes and incidents and in the poetic re-creation of them for their original tone and value. One passage at a time was the rule. This period was followed by a transitional one in which numerous citations or allusions were combined together. Each member of the combination, however, continued to be used in its natural and original sense. Then came the allegorical stage in which scripture phrases and statements were brought under the moulding and controlling hand of an extra-scriptural conception. After that followed the period of bitter, cynical, and pessimistic use, somewhat relieved by the power of the drama to take the poet outside of himself into the life of another age and to re-create for it characters, conflicts, and crises. Finally came a return of the quiet faith of the first period. But the sixth period is markedly different from the first. The change is indicated by the different artistic and personal attitude toward Scripture more clearly than in any other way. In *In Memoriam* Tennyson was not over-friendly toward a faith which had center everywhere nor cared to fix itself to form.[1] The poet's heart cherished a definite faith of a definite form and in a definite person. As his life verged toward its close and the long fruit of imaginative living in many and varied characters became mature, the definite was felt to be a part of the indefi-

---

[1] *In Memoriam*, XXXIII.

nite, and a great vastness made itself increasingly felt behind the local and the historic. The reality and truth of the lesser visions were not abandoned, but their concrete images, even while they were retained, were fused with more universal ones. The difference is difficult to express, but a few contrasts may make it appear at least partially. *In Memoriam* depicts delight in a vision of Hallam and the poet dying at the same time:

> And he that died in Holy Land
> Would reach us out the shining hand
> And take us as a single soul.[2]

Crossing the Bar voices a similar hope. The poet expects to see his Pilot face to face when he has crossed the bar. In both cases there is a meeting, directly after death, with a personal Being and Friend. "Face to face" seems, at least vaguely, to suggest the biblical phrase. But the "Pilot" is not a scriptural character, nor is the harbor imagery that surrounds him to be found in the Bible. He is outside "our bourne of Time and Place." "That Divine and Unseen Who is always guiding us"[3] may be used with entire truthfulness to describe Christ. But in itself the expression is too large to have any necessary historical connection. It belongs to the dialect of Universal Religion. It is significant that the poet wished this poem to be placed last in every edition of his works.[4]

The Ancient Sage has been called "a later *Two Voices*."[5] The whole poem is very personal.[6] The two poems present essentially the same problem and essentially the same solution: How is the materialistic evidence of the senses to be refuted? *The Two Voices* cites the evidence of consciousness because of which man "doubts against the sense" and has the conception of eternity in his soul. *The Ancient Sage* in like manner says that the Nameless speaks within the soul, and that man sees

---

[2] *In Memoriam*, LXXXIV.
[3] *Memoir*, II, 367.
[4] *Memoir*, II, 367.
[5] Stopford Brooke, *Tennyson, etc.*, p. 463.
[6] *Memoir*, II, 319.

him when he sends his soul thru the boundless heaven.[7]   The
practical lesson in *The Two Voices* is that man should heed
the better voice which says " Rejoice! Rejoice!" [8]   *The Ancient Sage* also says " Cleave ever to the sunnier side of doubt."[9]
The real difference between the two poems, aside from the
naturally greater and richer power of thought, is best seen by
noting the scripture allusions in *The Two Voices,* and by the
fact that there are no such allusions in *The Ancient Sage.*   The
sage is dated " a thousand years before the time of Christ " just
in order to free him from all historic environments.   By contrast
the beautiful portraiture of Stephen in *The Two Voices* and
the numerous other clear biblical allusions had their reason
in the early simplicity of the first period in its relation to the
Bible.   *The Ancient Sage* has at least as much faith as is
reached in *The Two Voices,* but the former indicates the difference when the young man is entreated to " cling to faith beyond
the forms of faith." [10]

Years bring the philosophic mind.   For Tennyson they
brought also a change not only from theologic but also from
scriptural imaginations to philosophic ones.   *Akbar's Dream*
was close to the heart of Tennyson's later years.[11]   Akbar
reigned in the sixteenth century after Christ.   The poem
might contain, without anachronism, allusions to biblical matter,
and actually does include some such lines.   Technically it is
not scriptureless.   But Akbar aims to gather from the king's
great garden the choicest-grown blossom of each fair plant.   He
will wreathe out of them all a crown for Brahmin, Buddhist,
Christian, and Parsee.   The fairness of all the flowers must
make one fairness.   Akbar's universal religion includes not
only the best in all others, but also in that of Issa Ben Mariam.
The Christian bell, the minaret-cry, and even the vaguer voices
of polytheism must make one music.   Akbar, in fact, rejoices

[7] *The Ancient Sage,* 31-34, 47-49.
[8] *The Two Voices,* 462.
[9] *The Ancient Sage,* 68.
[10] *The Ancient Sage,* 69.
[11] *Memoir,* II, 388 f., 398.

in the thought that the Divine Being, who himself shaped all
forms and ceremonies that existed on earth before he came to
it, himself obeyed them when he came from beyond the bridge
that connects us with the infinite. If, here again, what Akbar
says of forms is compared with what *In Memoriam* says of them
in the passage already referred to, it will be seen that the
former is the universalizing of the latter and thus includes it.[12]
It is to be noted that altho Akbar's eclectic religion hopes to
unite all creeds, castes, and peoples, he has a bad dream. In
the dream he rears

> a sacred fane,
> A temple, neither Pagod, Mosque, nor Church,
> But loftier, simpler, always open-door'd
> To every breath from heaven, and Truth and Peace
> And Love and Justice came and dwelt therein.[13]

He and his beloved chronicler, however, are slain. But the
dream allows him, after death, to watch his successors loosen
stone from stone till from the ruin the old shriek and curse
arise again. The significant point is that still later Akbar
sees Christian missionaries restore the temple. That is: Christianity is not so much a new temple as the re-creation, stone
for stone, of the ideal and universal faith of the human race.
That ideal faith of the heart of man might be held by some
ancient sage " a thousand years before the time of Christ," or
by some great eclectic fifteen hundred years after Him, or in
the day of Christ Himself. It was liable to more or less perfect embodiment at various times and places and also to more
or less ruinous temporary destructions. These constituted the
historical and local side of the matter. Christianity must not
be thought of as the exclusive and only perfect faith. It was,
indeed, the great, practical, re-creative force. But the ideal
religion must not be conceived of as absent from the dreams
of those who never knew Jesus or of those who sought to blend
him with other faiths.

---

[12] *Akbar's Dream*, 125-146; *In Memoriam*, XXXIII.
[13] *Akbar's Dream*, 170-174.

Tennyson's religion may, perhaps, like his artistic growth, be illuminated by his progressive relationship to Scripture as seen in his poems. From this point of view it is not a fixed element to be crystallized out of an inductive study of his productions. It is a growing and a becoming like his artistic use of Scripture. Critics affirm that he had a definite religious faith, which must be distinguished from the indifference of Keats and the unbelief of Shelley on the one hand, and from the exact dogmatics of Milton, Byron, and Browning on the other.[14] They state that he held something like a creed at least with reference to the incarnation, prayer, and immortality. The *Memoir* itself declares that the poet always said he had a creed but would not formulate it, for the people would not understand him if he did. He referred men to his poems.[15] It is not in the purpose of this study to do more. The great poet's fundamental principles probably never underwent any marked change in their essential quality. But they spread at last from the Bible as a center of expression to the circumference of religious humanity at large. This is the meaning of the Period of Disuse.

There is an analogy in this matter between Tennyson and Shakespeare. The statement of the *Memoir,* in speaking of the disposition of the body of the poet in the coffin, that *Cymbeline* was placed with it connotes fine insight as well as filial piety. For *Cymbeline* harmonizes well with Tennyson's final faith. It is technically scriptureless. It comes from Shakespeare's ripened and mellow years. The bitterness and pessimism of *Macbeth* are overpast. The presiding deity makes all things work together for good. A spirit of generous forgiveness reigns in Cymbeline's own soul at the close. Tho living in the first century he condemns no one to death when he reaches his hour of authority. Jupiter gives him largeness of heart. Altho victorious over Rome he will pay tribute to her. All suffering is seen as disciplinary, the expression of

---

[14] Stopford Brooke, *op. cit.*, pp. 13-30.
[15] *Memoir*, I, 308-327.

an active Divine Love. It may not be safe to trust the genuineness of the rimed speech of Jupiter. If it were, "whom best I love I cross" would be a fine pagan parallel to "whom the Lord loveth he chasteneth." [16] In any case the speech expresses the spirit of the play. Doubtless Tennyson loved *Cymbeline* in part because it makes the native Briton, even in the state of wildness, superior to the Roman in honesty, directness, and courage. Imogen, too, is an ideal of womanly character. But its most endearing quality, the quality that made the laureate want it in his last days, was probably its calmly universalized sense of an overruling power, which blends the sufferings and enigmas of life into a discipline of immortal and ageless Love. The play was doubtless 'very personal' to Shakespeare in his later period and for the same reasons to Tennyson in his closing years. Like his own *Ancient Sage* it spoke to him of a timeless, ungeographic, and spiritual world. Combining of biblical phrases, biblical allegorizing, and even biblical satire, were stages of earlier development. The simplicity of the first period was reborn. But it was more than a re-birth. It was no longer a thing of separate bright scripture colors each of which could be identified and named. It was the shining, toward evening, of a full and broad white ray which blended into itself all the true colors of the spectrum, but in which no one of them could be separately seen.

---

[16] *Cymbeline*, v, iv, 101; *Hebrews*, XII, 5-11.